R. H. Parker

Understanding Company
Financial Statements

Fourth Edition

PENGUIN BOOKS

For Theresa and Michael

Acknowledgements
For 'The Hardship of Accounting' from *The Poetry of Robert Frost*,
edited by Edward Connery Lathem: to the Estate of Robert Frost,
Edward Connery Lathem and to Jonathan Cape Ltd. Copyright 1936 by Robert Frost.
Copyright © 1964 by Lesley Frost Ballantine. Copyright © 1969 by Holt.
Rinehart & Winston, Inc. Reprinted by permission of Holt, Rinehart
& Winston, Inc.

PENGUIN BOOKS

Published by the Penguin Group
Penguin Books Ltd, 27 Wrights Lane, London W8 5TZ, England
Penguin Books USA Inc., 375 Hudson Street, New York, New York 10014, USA
Penguin Books Australia Ltd, Ringwood, Victoria, Australia
Penguin Books Canada Ltd, 10 Alcorn Avenue, Toronto, Ontario, Canada M4V 3B2
Penguin Books (NZ) Ltd, 182–190 Wairau Road, Auckland 10, New Zealand

Penguin Books Ltd, Registered Offices: Harmondsworth, Middlesex, England

First published 1972
Second edition 1982
Third edition 1988
Fourth edition 1994
10 9 8 7 6 5 4 3

Copyright © R. H. Parker, 1972, 1982, 1988, 1994
All rights reserved

The moral right of the author has been asserted

Typeset by Datix International Limited, Bungay, Suffolk
Printed in England by Clays Ltd, St Ives plc
Filmset in 10/12 pt Monophoto Bembo

Contents

Preface to the Fourth Edition

An eminent company lawyer has written of the published financial statements of companies that 'to the average investor or creditor – "the man on the Clapham omnibus" – they are cryptograms which he is incapable of solving'.* This small book is an attempt to make the task easier. It is written for the general reader and the first-year student, not for my fellow accountants, and does not pretend to be more than an introduction to a difficult subject. No previous knowledge is assumed. The emphasis is on analysis and interpretation rather than accounting techniques. Special attention has been paid to making the language of accounting and finance intelligible to the lay person.

The previous editions of this book were published in 1972, 1982 and 1988. The fourth edition retains the general approach of these editions, but once again the pace of change has been so fast that much has had to be rewritten.

I am greatly indebted to British Vita PLC for allowing me to reprint its 1992 annual report and its 1993 interim report. I am grateful to Mr K. R. Bhatt of British Vita, and to Professors T. E. Cooke and C. W. Nobes for valuable comments on previous drafts of the manuscript, but any errors and misinterpretations that may remain are, of course, my responsibility.

My thanks also to my indefatigable secretary, Mrs Sylvia Jones, for much word processing.

* *Gower's Principles of Modern Company Law*, Stevens, 4th edn, 1979, p. 507.

1. Companies and Their Reports

In sooth a goodly company.

Revd Richard Harris Barham,
'The Jackdaw of Rheims'

Purpose and Design of the Book

The purpose of this book is to show the reader how to understand, analyse and interpret the reports sent by companies to their shareholders, and more especially the financial statements contained in them. In order to do this, we shall look in detail at the 1992 annual report of the British Vita group. We shall also refer occasionally to British Vita's 1991 and earlier reports and to the reports of other companies.

In this first chapter we survey in general terms the contents of a company annual report and look briefly at the nature and constitution of the limited liability company. Chapter 2 describes the various financial statements and introduces many important financial and accounting concepts. This is a vital chapter, providing the basis for the analysis which appears later in the book. Chapter 3 explains as briefly as possible the nature of company taxation and the function of the auditors. Chapter 4 deals with regulation, formats, accounting standards and inflation. Chapter 5 describes certain tools of analysis. Chapter 6 is concerned with profitability and return on investment, Chapter 7 with liquidity and cash flows, and Chapter 8 with sources of funds and capital structure. Chapter 9 summarizes the whole book.

Finance and accounting are specialist subjects. This does not mean that they need remain incomprehensible to the lay person. It does mean, however, that technical terms cannot entirely be avoided. One cannot, after all, learn to drive a car or play a piano without learning some new words. In order to make the learning process as painless as possible, technical terms are explained as they are introduced or shortly thereafter, and a glossary is provided for reference (Appendix B). It is hoped that some readers will want to know more about finance and accounting after reading this book. For such readers the references given in Chapter 9 should be useful.

Contents of a Company Annual Report

The 1992 annual report and accounts of British Vita PLC are reproduced as Appendix C by kind permission of the company. The original has a page size about twice that of the reproduction. The content of British Vita's report is typical of that of most listed companies. To get some idea of this content, it is worth leafing quickly through it.

What is the British Vita group and what do the member companies of it do? The group's own succinct description of itself is that the companies in the group are international leaders in foam, fibre, fabric and polymeric products. The principal activities listed in the Directors' Report [p. 17]* are

the manufacture and processing of polymers including cellular foams, synthetic fibre fillings, specialised and coated textiles, polymeric compounds and mouldings and engineering thermoplastics. It also has interests in the licensing of advanced technical processes.

The Operations Review [pp. 8–16] gives further details.

British Vita PLC, of Middleton, near Manchester, is the parent company of the group. There are fifteen wholly owned subsidiaries operating in the UK, as well as thirty-four continental European subsidiaries, in some of which there are minority shareholdings and one subsidiary each in the United States, Australia and Zimbabwe [pp. 42–3]. The group also has nine associated undertakings [p. 44].

Turning back to the beginning of the report, we find first of all the results for 1992 (with comparative figures for 1991) in the form

---

* All references in square brackets are to pages in Appendix C.

of Financial Highlights, that is, in summarized form [p. 1]. This is followed by the Chairman's Review [pp. 2–3]. Such a review, although not required by law, is published by almost all companies listed on the Stock Exchange. The content varies considerably. That of British Vita for 1992 looks both at the immediate past and at prospects for the future. Research has shown that this is one of the most widely read sections of an annual report, no doubt because it is presented in non-technical language and also, unlike most of the report, deals with the future as well as the past.

Pages 4 and 5 provide a Summary of Financial Data 1988–1992. Page 6 provides information about the directors and officers of the company, including potted biographies. The board of directors consists both of executive directors and non-executive directors, with the positions of chairman and chief executive held, as in most but not all listed companies, by different persons. Pages 8–16 provide a review of operations. This is a valuable section as it provides information on the group's various product lines and operations. At the time of writing there are proposals for companies to publish a more uniform operating and financial review.

The Directors' Report [pp. 17–21] is, unlike the Chairman's Review and the Operations Review, a statutory document whose contents are largely, but not wholly, determined by law (there is a summary of the legal requirements in the Glossary). The main topics dealt with in British Vita's 1992 report are profit and dividends, principal activities, fixed assets, subsidiary and associated undertakings, corporate governance, directors' and other interests, share capital, personnel, donations and auditors.

There now follows the most important and, for many, the most difficult section of the report: the financial statements [pp. 22–41]. These consist of a consolidated profit and loss account, two balance sheets (one for the group and one for the parent company), a group cash flow statement, a list of accounting policies (see Chapter 4) and fifteen pages of detailed notes. All of these will be looked at more closely. For the moment it is enough to note that the consolidated profit and loss account shows the results of the operations of the British Vita *group of companies* for the year ended 31 December 1992; the group balance sheet shows the financial position of the *group* as at 31 December 1992; the parent balance sheet shows the financial position of the *parent company only* as at 31 December 1992; and the cash flow statement shows the cash flows of the *group* during the year ended 31 December 1992.

Pages 42–4 list the principal subsidiary and associated undertakings forming part of the British Vita group with a note of the country of incorporation and principal operation and of each undertaking's product or activities.

Page 45 contains the Directors' Responsibility Statement and the Auditors' Report. These are discussed in Chapter 3.

Pages 46–7 give notice of the annual general meeting of the shareholders of the company. Every company must by law hold such a meeting once a year with an interval of not more than fifteen months between meetings.

The ordinary business of the meeting is very formal:

1. To receive and consider the accounts and the reports of the directors for the year ended 31 December 1992.
2. To confirm the dividends paid and to declare a final dividend on the ordinary shares (dividends are recommended by the directors but approved and declared by the shareholders).
3, 4 and 5. To reappoint directors.
6. To reappoint the auditors and authorize the directors to fix their remuneration.

There is also an item of special business.

The final page of the annual report [p. 48] gives the address of its 'registered office' (its official address) and the names and addresses of the group's auditors, principal bankers, and registrar and share transfer office. It also sets out a financial calendar giving the approximate dates on which a preliminary announcement of results is made, the report and accounts circulated, the annual general meeting held, the interim report circulated, and dividend payments made.

In some previous annual reports, but not in 1992, British Vita also published current cost information and a value added statement.

Corporate Governance

Listed companies such as British Vita are owned by shareholders, most of whom take no part in the formulation of company strategy or the day-to-day operations of the company. This is delegated to a board of directors. Boards are given considerable freedom in the way companies are run and, except in times of crisis, are subject to very little interference from the shareholders. There is thus a divorce of ownership from control. The problems of accountability which arise from this were addressed in the Cadbury Committee Report on the Financial Aspects of Corporate Governance. The committee produced in 1992 a Code of Best Practice.

British Vita's Directors' Report [pp. 18–19] refers to this code and gives details of how the group is managed. There is a main board and a management board. The former, which consists of both executive and non-executive members, has responsibility for the formulation of corporate strategy, approval of acquisitions and major capital expenditure, and treasury policy. The latter, which comprises the executive directors plus several chairmen or managing directors of UK and European subsidiaries, controls day-to-day operations.

The alternative to the British unitary board of directors comprising both executives and non-executives is the two-tier board system found in some continental European countries in which the executives form a board of management which reports to a supervisory board of non-executives. This system has received little support from British business, mainly because it is thought to imply, as in Germany, worker representation on the supervisory board.

As already noted, details of the membership of British Vita's board of directors in 1992 are given on p. 6 of the Report together with potted biographies. The non-executives all have long experience and knowledge of the British Vita group. In 1993 two further non-executives were appointed to the board, both from outside the company and with extensive experience of other companies.

Details of the directors' emoluments are given in note 9 [pp. 29–30]. The information to be provided on this is governed by company legislation and is summarized in the Glossary (Appendix B to this book). The amounts are determined by a remuneration committee composed of the Chairman of the Board and all the non-executive directors. Details of directors' shareholdings are given in the Directors' Report [on p. 19].

Users of Published Accounts

Although published financial statements are formally for shareholders only, they are also of great interest to other users and in practice they are treated as general-purpose financial statements available to all users. *The Corporate Report*, a discussion paper issued by the Accounting Standards Committee in 1975, classifies these other users as employees, loan creditors, analyst advisers, business contacts (customers and suppliers), the government and the public. Many users are also likely to be 'stakeholders' in the company. Stakeholders can usefully be classified into primary stakeholders (the shareholders), who have an ownership interest in the company; secondary stakeholders (e.g., loan creditors, employees, business contacts and tax collectors), with a financial but not an ownership interest in the company; and tertiary stakeholders, who have no direct financial interest but who are affected, or believe themselves to be affected, by the way in which the company's resources are managed (e.g., persons affected by pollution caused or allegedly caused by the company's activities). It is British Vita's policy to make its annual report generally available and not to prepare statements specifically aimed at other users, especially as many of its employees are also shareholders. Many companies, however, prepare a special report for the employees (sometimes, but not always, distributed with the annual report). This report may emphasize the value added statement (see Chapters 2 and 6) rather than the profit and loss account, and contain information presented in a simpler and more graphic form. Many other users might benefit from simplified financial statements.

Memorandum and Articles of Association

Every company must have both a memorandum of association and articles of association. The main contents of the memorandum are the name of the company, the situation of the registered office, a list of the objects for which the company has been formed and a statement that the liability of the members is limited. The list of objects is important since a company cannot legally do anything which is beyond its powers (*ultra vires*). In practice the problem is avoided by listing every conceivable (and sometimes inconceivable) object that the company is ever likely to have.

The articles are the internal regulations of the company and usually deal with such matters as the rights of particular classes of shares, transfer of shares, powers and duties of directors, accounts, dividends, reserves and quorums for meetings of shareholders and directors. A model set of articles called Table A can be adopted in full or in a modified form.

Classification of Companies

The chief characteristics of a limited liability company are: a corporate personality distinct from that of its owners or shareholders; the limiting of the liability of the shareholders to the amount invested (which is not the case for a sole trader or partnership where personal assets are available to pay business debts); and, in principle at least, a perpetual life: companies are born but they do not have to die of old age.

It was not until 1844 that incorporation became possible other than by the slow and difficult process of a special Act of Parliament or a Royal Charter. It took another eleven years for incorporation by registration to be linked with limited liability, by the Limited Liability Act 1855. The foundations of modern British company law (and also that of Australia, Canada, New Zealand, South Africa and many other Commonwealth or former Commonwealth countries) were laid in the Companies Act 1862. The law has been continually revised since. At the time of writing, most of the companies legislation in force in Britain is contained in the Companies Act 1985 as amended in 1989. The European Commission has an active programme of company law harmonization, which has greatly affected British companies (see the section below on company law and the EC).

At 31 March 1993 there were about 960,600 companies registered in Great Britain of which about 11,700 (1.2 per cent) were public companies and about 948,900 (98.8 per cent) were private companies. In 1992–3 about 109,900 new companies were registered.*

To explain the differences between public and private companies it is necessary to look at the ways in which companies can be classified. A public company is one whose memorandum of association states that it is such, whose name ends with the words 'public limited company' or 'plc' (or, optionally, 'ccc' for companies registered in Wales) and which has a minimum authorized and allotted share capital, one quarter at least of which has been paid up. The minimum amount is set at present at £50,000. Any company which is not a public company is a private company. A private company is not permitted to issue shares or debentures to the public.

A public company does not *have* to make a public issue of shares or debentures; it simply has the right to do so. Thus only about 1,800 UK public companies are listed (quoted) on a stock exchange and the division between private and public companies is not the same as that between companies with listed shares and those with unlisted shares. It is a necessary but not a sufficient condition for listing that the company be a public company. British Vita PLC is both a public and a listed company.

The Companies Act 1985 also divides companies into large, medium and small, using as criteria balance sheet total, turnover and the average number of employees. Small and medium companies are exempted from filing certain data with the Registrar of Companies. The exemptions do not apply to financial statements sent to shareholders but, as noted in Chapter 4, listed companies have the option to send summary financial statements to their shareholders. This option has been taken up only by companies with a very large number of shareholders. British Vita has chosen

---

* Department of Trade and Industry, *Companies in 1992–3*, HMSO, 1993.

Table 1.1. Ownership of Company Shares

	1969 %	1975 %	1981 %	1989 %
Persons	47.4	37.5	28.2	21.3
Charities	2.1	2.3	2.2	2.0
Banks	1.7	0.7	0.3	0.9
Insurance companies	12.2	15.9	20.5	18.4
Pension funds	9.0	16.8	26.7	30.4
Unit trusts	2.9	4.1	3.6	5.9
Investment trusts and other financial institutions	10.1	10.5	6.8	3.2
Industrial and commercial companies	5.4	3.0	5.1	3.6
Public sector	2.6	3.6	3.0	2.0
Overseas sector	6.6	5.6	3.6	12.4
	100.0	100.0	100.0	100.0

Source. The Stock Exchange Survey of Share Ownership, Table 2.1b: Share Register Survey Report End 1989, HMSO, 1991.

not to issue such statements. All companies must have at least two shareholders; there is no maximum limit. At 31 December 1992, for example, British Gas PLC had 2,036,826 ordinary shareholders.* Not all shareholders are persons. Table 1.1 gives estimates of percentages of market value of shareholdings by sector of *beneficial* holder. Since shares can be held by a nominee, the beneficial holder is not necessarily the same as the registered holder of a share.

The main features to note are the steady fall in the percentage of shares held by persons and the steady rise in the holdings of what are known as institutional shareholders (in particular pension funds but also insurance companies, investment trusts, unit trusts and banks). Overseas holdings of British shares increased significantly in the 1980s.

Some companies voluntarily disclose shareholder statistics. These

---

* The distinction between shareholders and stockholders, and between shares and stock, is not of practical importance. The terms are increasingly used interchangeably.

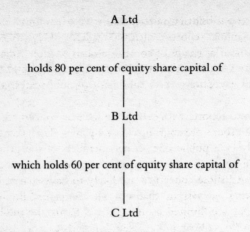

A Ltd

|

holds 80 per cent of equity share capital of

|

B Ltd

|

which holds 60 per cent of equity share capital of

|

C Ltd

may sometimes be difficult to interpret because of the existence of nominee shareholdings. At 31 December 1992 British Gas's shareholders held in total 4,310 million shares, so that the *average* holding was about 2,116 shares. The average institutional shareholding, however, was about 91,075 shares whereas the average individual holding was about 504 shares. Less than 2 per cent of the shareholders were institutions but they held nearly 77 per cent of the shares. Shareholdings of 3 per cent or over must be reported to a company by law. British Vita reports [p. 9] that apart from certain directors only the Prudential Corporation held more than 3 per cent of its issued share capital as at 8 March 1993.

The dominant form of business enterprise in the UK is not the individual undertaking but a group of undertakings (most but not necessarily all of which are companies) headed by what is known as a 'parent undertaking' which controls 'subsidiary undertakings' and significantly influences 'associated undertakings'. It is possible for a subsidiary itself to have subsidiaries. These are the sub-subsidiaries of the first parent undertaking. In the example above, A Ltd is the parent, B Ltd its subsidiary, and C Ltd its sub-subsidiary. Note that although A Ltd controls C Ltd its interest in its shares is only 48 per cent, i.e. 80 per cent of 60 per cent. Some parent undertakings exist purely to hold shares in operating subsidiaries. Others, like British Vita PLC, are operating companies as well.

The parent–subsidiary relationship is very common and practically all the annual reports which the reader is likely to be interested in will be those of *groups* of companies. It is possible for subsidiaries to hold shares in each other, but the Companies Act makes it illegal, with minor exceptions, for a subsidiary to hold shares in its parent company.

The annual reports with which we shall be concerned, then, will be those of groups or subgroups of companies. The parent company will usually be a public one. Other members of the group will be British public or private companies or companies incorporated overseas.* All those concerned are likely to have share capital. It is worth noting in passing that not all companies do have share capital. Some are 'limited by guarantee' (that is, the members have undertaken to contribute a fixed amount to the assets of the company in the event of its being wound up). The London School of Economics and Political Science is an example. Some companies are even unlimited; since these have the privilege of not publishing their accounts, they are not relevant to this book. They are used by professionals who desire corporate form but are not permitted to limit their liability, or by those who value the privilege of non-disclosure more than the limitation of liability (for example, the C & A department store). They have become more important since the Companies Act 1967 abolished 'exempt private companies' (essentially family companies exempt from publishing their accounts).

Company Law and the European Community

Most amendments to British company law from 1980 onwards are the result of implementing the company law 'directives' of the EC. Directives form part of UK law only when they have been

---

* The American equivalent of plc and Ltd is Inc. (i.e., incorporated). The nearest French, German and Dutch equivalents to a British public company are a *société anonyme* (SA), an *Aktiengesellschaft* (AG) and a *Naamloze Vennootschap* (NV); to our private companies, *société à responsabilité limitée* (SARL), *Gesellschaft mit beschränkter Haftung* (GmbH) and *Besloten Vennootschap* (BV).

incorporated into our domestic legislation. The most important directives so far as company financial reporting is concerned have been the fourth (on the accounts of individual companies), the seventh (on the accounts of groups) and the eighth (on auditors). It was the fourth directive that introduced into UK legislation standardized formats for financial statements (see Chapter 4) and a three-tier classification into large, medium and small companies.

Interim Reports

Twelve months is a long time to wait for information about the details of the financial progress of a company. It has therefore become increasingly common for major companies to issue unaudited interim reports at half-yearly and sometimes quarterly intervals. Listed companies are required by the Stock Exchange to circularize (or insert as a paid advertisement in two leading daily newspapers) a half-yearly interim report to shareholders not later than six months from the date of the notice calling an annual general meeting.

British Vita's interim report for the six months ended 30 June 1993 is reproduced in Appendix D. It comprises a chairman's statement, a consolidated profit and loss account, a group balance sheet and notes, which include a segmental analysis of turnover and operating profit. Interim reports give much less information than annual reports but they have grown in size in recent years.

It is, however, with the annual financial statements that this book is mainly concerned. Now that we have sufficient background information, they can be looked at in more detail.

2. The Financial Statements

The statements was interesting but tough.

Mark Twain,
The Adventures of Huckleberry Finn, Chapter 17

Assets, Liabilities and Shareholders' Funds

At the core of any company's annual report are the financial statements. Those for the British Vita group for the year ended 31 December 1992 are reproduced as Appendix C. We shall start by discussing the 1992 group balance sheet (the column of figures to the left on p. 24 of the appendix). This is a statement of the financial position of British Vita and its subsidiaries at 31 December 1992 as if they were one company.

Traditionally, British companies had the right to present a balance sheet in any way they pleased, so long as certain items were disclosed either on the face of the balance sheet or in the notes. As a result of the EC's fourth directive on company accounts, balance sheets are now more standardized in form (see Chapter 4). All company balance sheets, however, are built up from three main categories, namely, assets, liabilities and shareholders' funds. Assets can be defined as resources, tangible or intangible, from which future benefits are expected, and the benefits from which are controlled by a company as a result of a past transaction or other event. Most, but not all, assets are in the legal ownership of the company. Liabilities can be defined as obligations arising from past transactions or other events that involve the company in a probable future transfer of cash, goods or services. The relationship between the assets, liabilities and shareholders' funds can be looked at either from the point of view of shareholders (a 'proprietary' approach) or from the point of view of the company as a whole (an 'entity' approach). Two forms of the fundamental balance sheet identity can thus be derived:

> *Proprietary:* assets − liabilities = shareholders' funds
> *Entity:* assets = shareholders' funds + liabilities.

Very broadly, all that is being said is that, firstly, what a company owns *less* what a company owes is equal to the value of the shareholders' funds invested in it and that, secondly, what a company owns is financed partly by the owners (the shareholders) and partly by outsiders (the liabilities). Either way, a balance sheet must, by definition, balance. The useful accounting technique known as double entry ('debits' and 'credits') is based on these same identities (see Appendix A).

As we shall see in the next few sections, the three categories can each be subdivided: for example, shareholders' funds can be divided into share capital and reserves; assets into fixed assets and current assets; and liabilities into current liabilities (i.e., creditors falling due within one year), creditors falling due after more than one year and provisions for liabilities and charges.

British Vita has adopted a proprietary approach and presents its consolidated balance sheet in the form shown on p. 15 (see also Appendix C, p. 24).

Broadly, the capital and reserves are represented by the sum of the total assets less current liabilities, creditors falling due after more than one year and the provisions for liabilities and charges. (See below for an explanation of the minority interests item.)

The second important financial statement is the consolidated profit and loss account [p. 22]. While a balance sheet represents the financial position at a particular point in time, a profit and loss account (the American phrase is income statement) relates to a period, in this case the year ended 31 December 1992. It shows, from the point of view of the shareholders, the results of the year's activities. The British Vita group made sales (turnover) in 1992 of £788,528,000. The operating profit was £48,691,000; after addition of the share of profit of associated companies and deduction of interest payable, this figure rose to £55,156,000 (profit on ordinary

	£000
Fixed assets	238,123
Current assets	310,192
Creditors: amounts falling due within one year	(210,038)
Net current assets	100,154
Total assets less current liabilities	338,277
Creditors: amounts falling due after more than one year	(31,528)
Provisions for liabilities and charges	(22,183)
	284,566
Capital and reserves	281,575
Minority interests	2,991
	284,566

activities before taxation). This was reduced by taxation to £33,940,000 (profit on ordinary activities after taxation). After allowing for minority interests the profit for the year available for the shareholders came to £33,545,000. Out of this amount dividends have been or will be paid to the shareholders, amounting altogether to £15,296,000. This leaves £18,249,000 to be retained (ploughed back).

The group profit and loss account is drawn up from the point of view of the shareholders. A rather different view of the same figures can be gained by preparing a statement of value added. Unlike the balance sheet and the profit and loss account, this statement is not required by law. The philosophy behind it is that the group by its activities creates new wealth ('adds value'), which is then shared out among the employees, the providers of capital and the government, with a balance being retained to provide for the maintenance and expansion of assets.

Although British Vita, like many other companies, no longer publishes a statement of value added, it is possible to derive one so long as wages and salaries are disclosed. The necessary calculations are shown in Chapter 6. The statement given there demonstrates that gross value added was applied in 1992 as follows:

	%
Employees	69
Providers of capital:	
interest	3
dividends to British Vita shareholders	6
minority shareholders	0
Governments (as taxation)	7
Retentions for replacement and expansion:	
depreciation	9
retained profit	6
	——
	100

It is worth looking more closely at the link between the profit and loss account and the balance sheet. How can a company grow – that is, how can it increase its assets? Look again at the identity

$$\text{assets} = \text{liabilities} + \text{shareholders' funds.}$$

It is clear that the only ways to increase the assets are to increase the liabilities (to borrow) or to increase the shareholders' funds. How can a company increase the latter? There are two possibilities: it can issue more shares or it can plough back profits (assuming, of course, that it is making some). Ploughing back profits is the simplest but not necessarily the cheapest source of long-term finance for a company. Also, the more a company ploughs back the less, in the short run at least, there will be available for paying dividends.

The inflows and outflows of cash into a company are disclosed not in the balance sheet or profit and loss account but in a cash flow statement. This is required by an accounting standard, but not by law. In 1992 the British Vita group [p. 25] generated a net cash inflow from operating activities of £71,151,000. Since, as will be stressed in Chapter 7, increasing cash and making profits are not the same, this figure differs considerably from the operating profit of £48,691,000. A reconciliation is provided in note 22 [p. 40]. After allowing for net cash outflows relating to financial activities (mainly receiving and paying interest and dividends), taxation and investing activities (mainly purchasing tangible fixed assets and purchasing subsidiary undertakings) this was reduced to £4,287,000. Adding to this the net cash inflow from financing (mainly issuing shares and repaying loans), the result was an increase during the year in cash and cash equivalents of £57,891,000.

All three statements are linked to each other. The retained profit for the financial year forms part of the profit and loss account item in the balance sheet [see note 20, p. 39]. The increase in cash and cash equivalents is related to the movement during the year in the cash at bank and short-term investments item in the balance sheet [see note 23, p. 40].

Current Assets, Current Liabilities and Working Capital

Current assets comprise those assets which are not intended for continuing use in the business. They consist mainly of cash or items such as debtors and stocks which can normally be expected to be turned into cash within one year from the date of the balance sheet. The British Vita group at 31 December 1992 had current assets valued at £310,192,000, comprising stocks ('inventories' in US terminology) of £67,678,000, debtors ('accounts receivable') of £141,266,000 and cash at bank and short-term investments of £101,248,000. The figure for stocks may vary according to the rules of valuation adopted. British Vita's policy is set out as follows [p. 26]:

Stocks are valued at the lower of first-in, first-out cost and net realizable value; cost includes appropriate production overhead expenses.

The use of the lower of cost or net realizable value (that is, expected selling price net of selling expenses) is standard practice in Britain. The phrase 'first-in, first-out' (FIFO) refers to the assumption that the stocks acquired first have been sold or used up first. An alternative assumption, last-in, first-out (LIFO), is popular in the USA but rare in Britain. The cost of finished goods includes not only raw materials and direct labour but also production overheads (but not administrative or distribution overheads). In note 13 [p. 35] the group's stocks are analysed into raw materials and consumable stores on the one hand (56 per cent) and work in progress and finished goods (44 per cent) on the other. These percentages reflect the bulkiness of the finished products, stocks of which, especially in the parent company, are kept at a minimum.

The debtors figure is usually net of an allowance (or provision) for doubtful debts. Cash at bank may be thought to present no problem of valuation, but where it is held overseas and cannot easily be remitted its value in sterling may be uncertain. The general problem of foreign currency accounting is discussed further in Chapter 4.

Current liabilities are also described in the group balance sheet as 'creditors: amounts falling due within one year'. The group's current liabilities of £210,038,000 at 31 December 1992 are analysed in note 15 [p. 35]. The most important are trade creditors (i.e., amounts owing to suppliers) of £101,863,000, bank overdrafts of £23,292,000, corporation tax of £23,470,000, other taxes and social security costs of £10,646,000 and the proposed dividend of £7,811,000. Net current assets are also referred to as net working capital, or (more usually) just working capital. The relationship between current assets and current liabilities is very important and is discussed in detail in Chapter 7 on liquidity.

Fixed Assets

Fixed assets comprise those assets which are intended for use on a continuing basis for the purpose of the company's activities. Stocks, for example, are not regarded as fixed assets since they are acquired either for immediate resale (for example, cigarettes, as sold by a tobacconist) or as raw materials for use in manufacturing operations, or are the finished or partly finished ('work in progress') results of such operations. It is intention that determines whether an asset is fixed or not. Plant and vehicles, for example, are the *current* assets of a company whose business it is to manufacture them for sale.

It will be seen from the group balance sheet and notes 11 and 12 [pp. 32–4] that the net book values of the fixed assets of the British Vita group at 31 December 1992 were as follows:

	£000	£000
Tangible fixed assets:		
land and buildings	115,604	
plant and vehicles	102,418	
		218,022
Investments in:		
listed associated undertakings	9,430	
unlisted associated undertakings	10,671	
		20,101
Total		238,123

Tangible Fixed Assets

British Vita's fixed assets are of two kinds: tangible fixed assets and investments. Note 11 [p. 32] reveals that the plant and vehicles are shown at cost and the land and buildings at a valuation made in 1992. 'Cost' in accounting has usually meant the historical cost of acquisition or manufacture (if the asset was made by the company for its own use). Historical cost has been favoured by accountants because it is thought to be objective and verifiable by an independent third party such as an auditor. It can, however, get seriously out of line with current market values, especially in times of inflation. British Vita discloses that, had their land and buildings not been revalued, they would have been stated in the group balance sheet at a net book value of £82,640,000 instead of £115,604,000.

In accordance with the Companies Act, British Vita provides a breakdown of its land and buildings into freehold, long leasehold and buildings subject to finance leases.

Depreciation

The concept of depreciation means different things to different people, but in an accounting context it normally means spreading the net cost (sometimes after adjustment or revaluation) of a fixed asset over its estimated useful economic life. British Vita explains its policy as follows [p. 26]:

Depreciation of tangible fixed assets is provided at rates estimated to write off the cost or valuation of assets over their useful lives, the principal rates of annual straight line depreciation being:

(a) Freehold buildings 2½ per cent. Freehold land is not depreciated.
(b) Leasehold land and buildings 2½ per cent or over the period of the lease if less than forty years.
(c) Plant between 10 per cent and 33⅓ per cent.
(d) Vehicles between 16 per cent and 25 per cent.

$$\frac{Cost - Scrap\ value}{Year}$$

British Vita thus uses the straight line method of depreciation. Under this method the cost less estimated scrap value of a fixed asset is divided by the number of years of its estimated useful life. If, for example, a machine costs £1,200 and is expected to have a scrap value of £130 at the end of an estimated useful life of ten years, the annual depreciation using this method will be £1,070 ÷ 10 = £107.

Less popular but still quite common in Britain is the reducing balance method of depreciation. As the name implies, the amount of depreciation charged each year under this method decreases over the life of the asset. If, for example, a rate of 20 per cent were chosen for the asset which costs £1,200, the annual depreciation charges would be calculated as shown on p. 21.

The machine has been written down to its approximate scrap value. The correct percentage can be found by trial and error or by use of the formula

$$1 - \sqrt[n]{\frac{s}{c}}$$

where n is the number of years, s the estimated scrap value and c the cost. In this case

$$1 - \sqrt[10]{\frac{130}{1200}} = 0.2.$$

The charging of depreciation simultaneously reduces the recorded amount of the fixed asset and reduces net profit.

For the year ended 31 December 1992 the group charged against profits £25,001,000 of depreciation [note 2, p. 27]. The amounts given for the fixed assets in the group balance sheet are net of all accumulated depreciation, not only that of the current year but of all previous years since the purchase of the assets concerned.

		£
Cost		1,200
Year 1	Depreciation 20% of £1,200	240
		960
Year 2	Depreciation 20% of £960	192
		768
Year 3	Depreciation 20% of £768	154
		614
Year 4	Depreciation 20% of £614	123
		491
Year 5	Depreciation 20% of £491	98
		393
Year 6	Depreciation 20% of £393	79
		314
Year 7	Depreciation 20% of £314	63
		251
Year 8	Depreciation 20% of £251	50
		201
Year 9	Depreciation 20% of £201	40
		161
Year 10	Depreciation 20% of £161	32
		£129

Fixed Asset Investments

British Vita has a substantial investment in associated undertakings [p. 33]. The shares of these are valued in the company's own accounts at cost less amounts written off, but this is increased in the *group* balance sheet to include a proportionate share of their reserves (retained profits) since acquisition. This accounting treatment, which differs from that used for a subsidiary, is known as the 'equity method'.

As for associated companies, the shares of subsidiaries in a *parent company* balance sheet are valued at cost less amounts written off.

The shares of most subsidiaries, however, are eliminated from group balance sheets and replaced by their underlying assets and liabilities. Subsidiaries may be excluded from consolidation if their inclusion would not make a material difference or would cause disproportionate expense or undue delay. In rare circumstances they must be excluded. When so excluded, their shares are nevertheless included as investments, valued at cost less amounts written off.

Intangible Fixed Assets

A third category of fixed asset, which is not represented in British Vita's balance sheet, is the intangible fixed asset. This is a non-monetary fixed asset which is without physical substance. This category of asset includes not only such 'identifiable' intangibles as patents, trade marks and copyrights (see Glossary), but also goodwill. Brands are intangible assets regarded by some accountants as separately identifiable but by others as part of goodwill.

A company is not just a collection of tangible assets. It is, or should be, a going concern whose total value, by reason of its proven ability to earn profits, is greater than the sum of its parts. It is the difference between the total value and the sum of the parts which constitutes goodwill. It should not be regarded as in any way a fictitious asset: to be valuable, an asset does not have to be tangible. Goodwill is, however, very difficult to value objectively and company law does not permit it to appear in a balance sheet unless it has been purchased, and even then it is usually written off either immediately or quite quickly. In some group balance sheets an item appears entitled 'goodwill arising on consolidation' or 'goodwill on acquisition'. This represents the excess of the cost of shares in subsidiary companies over the book value of their net tangible assets at the date of acquisition; that is, the parent company was willing to pay more to purchase a company than the sum of its tangible fixed and net current assets. British Vita writes off goodwill on acquisition to reserves [p. 26, para. 2]. The cumulative amount of goodwill resulting from acquisitions in 1992 and earlier financial years amounts to £24,772,000 [note 20, p. 39].

Loans and Other Borrowings

The item 'Creditors: amounts falling due after more than one year' in British Vita's group balance sheet represents the extent to which the group, not wishing to obtain further long-term funds from its shareholders, has borrowed from outsiders, both in the UK and overseas. Details are given in notes 16 and 17 [pp. 36–7]. The major part consists of loans both long-term (not wholly repayable within five years) and medium-term (repayable within five years). The proportion of the loans payable within one year is included under the heading 'Creditors: amounts falling due within one year'.

Banks are an obvious source of outside finance and most of British Vita's borrowings are in the form of bank loans. These are not the only forms of borrowing. The BICC Group, for example, has debenture stock secured by a floating charge and unsecured debentures. The word 'debenture' simply refers to a document providing evidence of a long-term borrowing or loan. Debentures are usually, but not necessarily, secured on the assets of the company, in which case they may be known as mortgage debentures. If a company fails in its obligation to pay interest or repay the loan, the secured property of the company can be sold in order to provide the necessary funds. The phrase 'unsecured debenture' is unusual, 'unsecured loan' often being preferred. 'Debenture stock' results from the fact that instead of issuing individual debentures the company has created one loan fund to be divided among a class of lenders, each of whom will receive a debenture stock certificate. Companies may, and often do, make more than one issue of debentures, the terms of issue and, in particular, the rate of interest varying according to the financial circumstances of the time. Such issues may be made at par (that is, at face value), at a discount (less than face value) or at a premium (more than face value). Issue at a discount increases the effective interest rate payable; issue at a premium (which is rare) reduces it. Issues are often made at a discount in order to keep the interest rate on the par value (known as the coupon rate) a reasonably round figure, while allowing the effective rate to be adjusted more finely.

Debentures and loans may be secured by a fixed charge on a

particular asset or by a floating charge on all the assets or particular classes of assets. A floating charge, unlike a fixed charge, allows a company to dispose of the assets charged in the usual course of business without obtaining special permission from the lender. Stock-in-trade is a particularly suitable asset to be charged in this manner. If assets are, or may be, used as security for more than one loan, it is necessary to state the order of priority of the lenders (for example, debenture stock may be stated to be secured by a *first* floating charge).

Some debentures are irredeemable – that is, they will never have to be repaid (unless the company is wound up) – but most are redeemable. It is common not only to specify the latest date, but also to give the company the power to redeem earlier if it so wishes. This is especially useful if debentures are issued in times of high interest rates and if there is an expectation of lower rates later.

In principle there is a clear distinction between borrowings and shareholders' funds. In practice, especially in recent years, the distinction has become blurred by the issue by some companies of 'hybrid' securities – securities with the characteristics of both debt and equity. There has also been an increase in 'off balance sheet finance', that is, borrowing in such a fashion that the debt does not appear as a balance sheet item. Standard accounting practice does not permit the exclusion from the balance sheet of finance leases, long-term contracts allowing the company the use, but not the ownership, of an asset in return for a periodic rental. British Vita includes finance leases as part of its borrowings [note 16, p. 36]. Both leasing and off balance sheet financing are discussed further in Chapter 8.

How much to borrow, and when and in what form to do so are vital matters to any company. We shall look at these problems in Chapter 8.

Provisions for Liabilities and Charges

Provisions for liabilities and charges are defined as amounts retained as reasonably necessary for the purpose of providing for any liability or loss which is either likely to be incurred or certain to be incurred, but uncertain as to amount or as to the date on which it will arise. The two most important provisions of this kind, as British Vita's note 18 [pp. 37–8] demonstrates, are for deferred taxation and for pensions. Deferred taxation is discussed in Chapter 3. Most companies provide pension benefits for their employees. British Vita's pension arrangements are set out at length in note 10 [p. 31].

Share Capital and Reserves

The shareholders' funds section of the group balance sheet is subdivided into share capital and reserves. Further details are given in notes 19 and 20 [pp. 38–9].

Shareholders differ from debenture-holders in three ways: they are members (owners) of the company, not lenders; they receive dividends (a share of the profits), not interest; and, except in special circumstances, the cost of their shares will not be repaid (redeemed) to them by their company. Listed shares can of course be sold to other investors on a stock exchange, but both the redemption of shares and the buying by a company of its own shares, although allowable subject to certain restrictions, are relatively uncommon in the UK.

There are two main types of shares: ordinary and preference. The difference between an ordinary shareholder and a preference shareholder is very important. The latter is usually entitled only to a dividend at a fixed rate (4.2 per cent in the case of British Vita), but has priority of repayment in the event of the company being wound up. This is not always so, however, and the exact rights must always be looked up in the company's articles of association. Preference shares may be cumulative or non-cumulative. British Vita's are cumulative, which means that if the company misses a dividend payment it carries it forward to the next year. Any arrears of preference dividends must be shown in a note to the balance sheet. Non-cumulative preference dividends, on the other hand, do not have to be carried forward.

The size of the dividends paid to ordinary shareholders varies according to the profits made by the company. It can be seen from note 6 [p. 28] that British Vita paid an interim ordinary dividend of 3.5 p per share during 1992 and that a final ordinary dividend of 3.65 p is proposed. The total ordinary dividend is thus 7.15 p. The par or face value of the ordinary shares is 25 p each [p. 38, note 19], and the total dividend could be described as a dividend of 28.6 per cent on the par value.

More important to an investor is the relationship between the dividend and the current *market* price of the share. This is known as the dividend yield and is discussed in Chapter 8 in the context of earnings yields and price–earnings ratios. For the moment, it should be noted that every share must have a par value* but that this is not necessarily the same as the issue price of the shares or their market price. Shares can be issued at more than their par value: this gives rise to a *share premium*. The British Vita group has a share premium of £81,228,000 [p. 39, note 20]. A share premium cannot be distributed, but it can be used to make a bonus or capitalization issue (see p. 104). Once a share has been issued, its market price fluctuates from day to day in accordance with supply and demand. If the shares can be bought and sold on a stock exchange, then the current market price can easily be found in the financial pages of a newspaper or from the *Stock Exchange Daily Official List*. The most complete newspaper list is given in the *Financial Times*. The information given in that paper's daily share information service is further discussed in Chapter 8.

A company does not have to issue all its shares at once, nor does it have to request full payment on the shares immediately. British Vita has authority to issue (that is, it has authorized capital of) 300,000,000 ordinary shares of 25 p each, and 60,000 4.2 per cent cumulative preference shares of £1 each [p. 38, note 19]. As at 31 December 1992 it had issued 213,926,954 ordinary shares (par value £53,481,738) and 57,450 preference shares (par value £57,450). All the shares are described as being fully paid; that is, the company does not have the right to call up any further amounts from the shareholders. They could have been partly paid. For example, a 25 p share could be payable 5 p on application for the shares, a further

---

* No-par-value shares are common in North America but illegal in the UK.

5 p on allotment, when the directors decide to whom the shares are going to be issued (or 'allotted'), and the remaining 15 p in calls. Thus, in summary, one can distinguish authorized, issued, called-up and paid-up share capital.

In 1992 British Vita increased its issued ordinary share capital in three ways: by means of a rights issue (see Chapter 8) in which 35,416,471 new shares of 25 p par value were issued at 212 p each, to provide financing for future acquisitions and investments; by the allotment of 1,353,649 new shares, fully paid, in accordance with the rules of the employee share option schemes; and by the allotment of 80,609 shares, fully paid, to subscribers to the company's personal equity plans (PEPs). In order for these issues to be made the company's authorized ordinary share capital was increased from £60 million (240 million shares) to £75 million (300 million shares).

Details of the group's reserves are given in note 20 [p. 39]. The Companies Act distinguishes for a *company* between 'distributable' and 'undistributable' reserves. The former comprises realized profits less realized losses. British Vita's group profit and loss account balance of £125,745,000 is regarded by the company as distributable. The share premium account, revaluation reserve (created as a result of the revaluation of fixed assets on the other side of the balance sheet), and other reserves, totalling altogether £102,291,000, are not so regarded. The movements on reserves during the year included the increase in share premium resulting from the share issues; the surplus arising on the revaluation of land and buildings; the increase in the retained profit; and the write-off of goodwill arising on acquisitions.

It is very important not to confuse reserves with cash. To say that a company has large reserves is not the same thing as saying that it has plenty of cash. If a company has reserves it must have net assets of equal amount, but these assets may be of any kind (e.g., machinery, stock-in-trade). Thus it is perfectly possible (and often sensible) for a company to have both large reserves and a large bank overdraft.

Consolidated Profit and Loss Account

British Vita's consolidated profit and loss account is given on pages 22 and 23 of its annual report. It follows the most popular of the four formats permitted by the Companies Act (see Chapter 4) and summarizes the year's operations from the point of view of the shareholders.

The first item in the profit and loss account is turnover (£788,528,000). This represents the net amounts invoiced to external customers by companies in the group but excludes value added taxes and sales taxes and the sales of the associated undertakings [p. 26]. Turnover within the group is not included, since to do so would merely inflate both sales and purchases. Note 1 [p. 27] analyses turnover by class of business and by geographical origin and destination.

Cost of sales (£602,698,000) – that is, the cost of the goods sold during 1992 whether or not manufactured in 1992 – is deducted from turnover to give the gross profit (£185,830,000). From this are further deducted distribution costs (£48,310,000) and administrative expenses (£88,829,000) to give an operating profit of £48,691,000. Some of the more important constituents of cost of sales, distribution costs and administrative expenses are disclosed in notes 2 [p. 27], 8 and 9 [pp. 29–30]. From these notes we can discover total employment costs (£194,172,000), broken down into wages and salaries, social security costs and other pension costs, depreciation (£25,001,000) and the cost of hire and leasing of plant and vehicles (£3,043,000). Vehicles and plant may be hired and leased instead of owned (see Chapter 8). Either way, the group has the use of them – hence the law also requires disclosure of hire and leasing charges as well as depreciation. Details are also given of the directors' emoluments and the auditors' remuneration (see Chapter 3).

The next item is the group share of profits of associated undertakings. The accounting treatment of associated undertakings differs, as we have seen, from that of subsidiaries. Like the latter, the appropriate share of profit or loss before tax is brought into the group results

– not just the dividends received; but, unlike subsidiaries, it is brought in as one figure, not split into its component parts. This is because the group controls the sales, wages, etc., of its subsidiaries but not those of its associated undertakings. Nevertheless, British Vita discloses in note 3 [p. 28] its share of the turnover of its associated undertakings (£83,645,000), its share of the profits less losses, before and after tax (£5,623,000 and £4,098,000 respectively), and dividends receivable from them (£1,652,000). In the balance sheet, it will be remembered, the underlying assets and liabilities of an associated undertaking are *not* brought in (because they are not under British Vita's control), but instead the cost of the original investment is augmented by a share of the associated undertaking's retained profits since acquisition. For all the above items a split is provided between the amounts arising from acquisitions during the year and those not so arising.

The next item is interest (net) of £842,000, further details of which are given, in accordance with the Companies Act, in note 4 [p. 28].

It is now possible to calculate profit on ordinary activities before taxation (£55,156,000). Taxation (see Chapter 3) amounts to £21,216,000, so profit on ordinary activities after taxation is £33,940,000.

The profit after tax is not the same as the profit for the year attributable to shareholders. Two further items may need to be deducted: the share of the profit after tax which is attributable to the minority shareholders in the group (£395,000 in 1992); and 'extraordinary' items. British Vita records no extraordinary items in its 1992 accounts. Such items are now very rare because of the restrictive definition in the relevant accounting standard (see Chapter 4). Standard accounting practice distinguishes between extraordinary items and exceptional items. *Extraordinary items* are material items possessing a high degree of abnormality which arise from events or transactions that fall outside the ordinary activities of a business and which are not expected to recur. They can be profits or losses; the tax on them is shown separately. In contrast, *exceptional items* are material items which derive from events or transactions that fall within the ordinary activities of a business and which need to be disclosed by virtue of their size or incidence.

We have at last reached the profit for the financial year attributable to shareholders. This amounted to £33,545,000 in 1992. The remainder of the profit and loss account is concerned with the distribution or retention of this sum: £15,296,000 has been or will be distributed; £18,249,000 is to be retained. Details of dividends are given in note 6 [p. 28]. An interim dividend of £7,483,000 has already been distributed to the ordinary shareholders. A final dividend of £7,811,000 is proposed. The preference shareholders receive £2,000.

The profits retained are spread around the group: £3,213,000 in the books of the parent company, £12,590,000 in the books of the subsidiaries and £2,446,000 in the books of the associated companies (over whose dividend payment policies British Vita has significant influence but not control).

At the foot of the group profit and loss account a note is given of the earnings per ordinary share. Earnings per share (EPS) is based on earnings per *ordinary* share. The relevant figure for earnings was thus £33,543,000 in 1992 – the profit for the financial year less the preference dividends. EPS is not of interest to preference shareholders since their dividend is fixed irrespective of the level of earnings.

As at 31 December 1992 there were 213,926,954 shares [note 19, p. 38]. The EPS calculation is, however, based on the weighted average of ordinary shares in issue during the year, namely, 206,376,573 shares [note 7, p. 29]. The calculation of EPS is thus:

$$\text{EPS} = \frac{33,543,000 \times 100}{206,376,573} \text{ p} = 16.3 \text{ p.}$$

The concept of earnings per share is discussed further in Chapter 8.

Profit earned needs to be related to investment made, and compared, if possible, with the performance of similar companies. Profitability and return on investment form the main subjects of Chapter 6.

The consolidated profit and loss account is followed [on p. 23] by three subsidiary statements: a statement of total recognized gains and losses; a note of historical cost profits and losses; and a reconciliation of movements in shareholders' funds. There is also reference to a statement of movements in reserves.

The purpose of the statement of total recognized gains and losses is to bring together those gains and losses which have been passed through the profit and loss account and those which have not; that is, the profit for the financial year (£33,545,000), the unrealized surplus on revaluation of properties (£5,231,000 – see note 20, p. 39) and the currency translation differences on foreign currency net investments (£15,704,000).

The note of historical cost profits and losses provides a calculation of what British Vita's profit on ordinary activities before taxation and retained profit for the financial year would have been if they had been based entirely on historical cost accounting without any revaluation of fixed assets. It can be seen that the main effect of the revaluations was to increase the depreciation charge so that the reported figures (£55,156,000 and £18,249,000) were slightly lower than they otherwise would have been (£55,446,000 and £18,539,000). The purpose of the statement is to facilitate inter-company comparisons: not all British companies revalue their assets and those that do may not do so every year or on a comparable basis.

The purpose of the reconciliation of movements in shareholders' funds is to explain how the total of shareholders' funds has changed during the year. For many companies in most years, and indeed for British Vita in 1991, the largest item is the retained profit (profit for the financial year less dividends). In 1992 for British Vita the largest item was new share capital subscribed. Shareholders' funds were also increased by other recognized gains and losses (net) and reduced by the write-off of goodwill.

Shareholders' funds is made up of share capital and reserves. A statement of movements in reserves is given in note 20 [p. 39]. From this can be seen how each reserve category (share premium account, revaluation reserve, other reserves, profit and loss account) changed during the year. The most important changes in 1992, as might be expected, were as a result of the retention of profit and the share premiums arising on the share issues.

Cash Flow Statement

A cash flow statement discloses a business's inflows and outflows of cash and 'cash equivalents' during an accounting period. Cash equivalents are short-term, highly liquid investments which are both readily convertible into known amounts of cash without notice, and were within three months of maturity when acquired, net of advances from banks repayable within three months from the date when the advance was made. In the UK, cash flow statements are required not by company law but by accounting standard (see Chapter 4). They may be prepared by the 'direct method' or the 'indirect method' (see below). Cash flows are classified under the following headings:

> operating activities
> returns on investment and servicing of finance
> taxation
> investing activities
> financing.

The statement concludes with the increase (decrease) in cash and cash equivalents during the year. Under the indirect method (used by British Vita), the cash flow from operating activities is calculated by adding back to operating profit any depreciation charged and increases/decreases in debtors, creditors and stocks. Details are given in note 22 [p. 40]. The more easily understood but less popular direct method reports, in classified form, the cash receipts and cash payments for each activity. The direct method is more straightforward than the indirect method but it lacks a link with the profit and loss account.

Cash flow statements have superseded the statement of source and application of funds (funds statements) previously required to be published. Funds statements emphasized working capital rather than cash flows. By definition cash flow statements exclude non-cash transactions. For this reason, the accounting standard also requires footnote disclosure of major non-cash transactions.

With this background we can now look at the cash flow statement of British Vita for 1992. In summary the cash inflows and outflows of the group in 1992 (arranged in order of importance) were as follows:

	£000	%
Cash inflows		
Issues of ordinary share capital	75,167	48
Net cash inflow from operating activities	71,151	46
Interest received	7,556	5
Other cash inflows (net of other cash outflows)	2,082	1
	155,956	100
Cash outflows		
Tangible fixed assets purchased	33,509	22
Net decrease in loans	20,830	13
Taxation paid	15,956	10
Dividends paid	13,860	9
Purchase of subsidiary undertakings	7,221	5
Interest paid	6,689	4
	98,065	63
Increase in cash and cash equivalents	57,891	37
	155,956	100

This summary shows that the most important sources of cash for the British Vita group in 1992 were the issue of new ordinary share capital and the net cash inflow from operations. As already noted, the latter should be clearly distinguished from the operating profit item in the consolidated profit and loss account. Operating profits are calculated not as cash is received or paid but as revenues or expenses are earned or incurred; that is, accrual accounting (see Chapter 4) is used, not cash accounting. Operating profits thus take account not just of increases and decreases in cash but also of depreciation and of changes in debtors, creditors and stocks. This is demonstrated in British Vita's note 22 [p. 40] which provides a reconciliation of the two concepts.

The most important uses of cash in 1992 were the purchase of new fixed assets, the repayment of loans, the payment of taxation, the payment of dividends, the purchase of subsidiary undertakings and the payment of interest. Further details of this last item are given in note 12 [p. 34]. The tax and dividend figures are not the same as those in the group profit and loss account, but represent tax *paid* and dividends *paid*. The latter figure (£13,860,000) is easily checked [note 6, p. 28]. It is equal to the proposed ordinary dividends of 1991 (£6,375,000) (which were not paid until 1992) plus 1992's interim ordinary dividend of £7,483,000 and the 1992 preference dividend of £2,000.

Depreciation and Cash Flow

In the cash flow statement [p. 25] cash inflows and cash outflows refer to movements in cash and cash equivalents. The term cash flow is also sometimes used, perhaps more by financial analysts than accountants, to mean net profit plus depreciation. A more accurate term for cash flow in this sense would be working capital from operating activities, since, unlike cash flow from operating activities, no adjustment is made for increases/decreases in debtors, creditors and stocks.

It is important to understand that depreciation is neither a cash inflow nor a cash outflow. The cash outflow obviously took place when the fixed asset was originally bought. It would be double counting to regard each year's depreciation as a further cash outflow.

Events after the Balance Sheet Date

Important events may sometimes take place between the date of the balance sheet (e.g., 31 December 1992) and the date on which the balance sheet is approved by the board of directors for publication (e.g., 9 March 1993). An event which does not provide additional evidence of conditions existing at the balance sheet date (e.g., the acquisition of a new subsidiary) is known as a 'non-adjusting event'. An example of an 'adjusting event', one which would require the financial statements to be altered if the amount was material, is the insolvency of a debtor as at the date of the balance sheet which only becomes known after the financial statements have been approved by the board.

Contingencies and Commitments

Company law requires the disclosure in the notes of contingent liabilities and capital commitments.

A contingency is a condition which exists at the balance sheet date, the outcome of which will be confirmed only on the occurrence or non-occurrence of one or more uncertain events. British Vita [p. 41, note 25] has a number of contingent liabilities; it has, for example, guaranteed some of the overdrafts and third-party liabilities of certain of its subsidiaries. It also has pension liabilities and contingent liabilities in respect of discounted bills of exchange. The company further reports that:

An action is being pursued in the USA against the Company and certain directors in relation to, and involving, Spartech Corporation [one of British Vita's subsidiaries], which is being vigorously defended as the directors are advised and believe there to be no merit in the claim.

Standard accounting practice also requires disclosure of probable contingent assets.

As required by law, British Vita discloses in note 21 [p. 39] its commitments for capital expenditure not provided for in the accounts and capital expenditure authorized by the directors but not contracted for. The reader of the annual report thus has knowledge of important projected cash outlays in the forthcoming period. Also reported in this note are the group's annual commitments in respect of operating leases and details of finance lease arrangements entered into. Leasing and the difference between operating and finance leases is discussed in Chapter 8.

3. Taxation and Audit

Taxation?
Wherein? And what taxation? My Lord Cardinal,
You that are blamed alike with us,
Know you of this taxation?

William Shakespeare,
King Henry the Eighth, I, ii

Never ask of money spent
Where the spender thinks it went
Nobody was ever meant
To remember or invent
What he did with every cent

Robert Frost,
'The Hardship of Accounting'

This chapter deals briefly with two important matters of which all readers of company reports should have some knowledge: taxation and audit. No attempt will be made to go into either in detail; company taxation in particular can become fearsomely complicated.

Taxation in the Accounts

There are references to several forms of taxation in British Vita's 1992 annual report and accounts. Taxation relating to the profit on ordinary activities for the year ended 31 December 1992 is stated in the consolidated profit and loss account to be £21,216,000, that is, 38 per cent of the profit on ordinary activities before taxation of £55,156,000. In the group balance sheet, the current liabilities (creditors: amounts falling due within one year) include corporation tax of £23,470,000 and other taxes and social security costs of £10,646,000 [note 15, p. 35]. The provisions for liabilities and charges include deferred taxation of £6,683,000. The cash flow statement shows taxation paid (£15,956,000). Further details of the company's tax position are given in note 5 [p. 28]. Turnover is stated to exclude value added tax [p. 26].

Corporation Tax

British companies pay corporation tax, not income tax. Taxable income is measured in much the same way as accounting profit, but with many exceptions, the major one being depreciation. The corporation tax rate is usually set annually in arrears for the financial year 1 April to 31 March. The tax is *assessed*, however, on the basis of a company's accounting period. British Vita's accounting period ends, it will be remembered, on 31 December each year. The tax is payable for most companies nine months after the end of the financial year in which the company's accounting period ends. The rate of corporation tax can vary. In the financial year 1992 (i.e., from 1 April 1992 to 31 March 1993) it was 33 per cent. The lower rate of 25 per cent applied to small profits.

When a dividend is paid by a company it pays advance corporation tax (ACT), an advance payment on the corporation tax liability, to the Inland Revenue. The amount paid has usually depended on the basic rate of income tax. Shareholders are taxed on the dividend grossed up at the basic rate, but receive a tax credit which can be set against their liability to income tax. The example on page 38, which assumes a corporation tax rate of 33 per cent and a basic rate of income tax of 25 per cent, shows how this 'imputation system', as it is called, worked in 1992/93.

The dividends paid or proposed do not include the tax credit and are shown in the company's accounts as the cash amounts received or receivable by the shareholders.

Suppose, in the example below, that the shareholder is a person (male), not a company, and holds all the shares. He would be assessed for income tax on £600, not £450. If he pays tax at 25 per cent, he can set off his tax credit of £150 against his liability to tax

	£000
Taxable profit	1,000
Corporation tax at 33%	330
Profit after tax	670
Dividend paid	450
Retained profit	220
ACT paid by company (25/75 × £450)	150
The shareholders receive:	
dividend	450
plus tax credit	150
	600

of the same amount. If he pays at more than 25 per cent, he has more to pay. A shareholder which is a company would treat such a dividend as 'franked investment income' and would not be assessed to corporation tax on it.

The company itself can normally (but not always, see below) recover the ACT paid (£150) by setting it off against its liability to corporation tax (£330) on its taxable profits. The difference (£180) is called 'mainstream' corporation tax.

The rules relating to ACT were made more complicated in 1993 when the link between the calculation of ACT and the basic rate of income tax was broken. Although the rates of corporation tax and income tax were not changed in 1993, the rate of ACT was reduced from 25/75ths to 9/31sts – from 25 per cent to 22.5 per cent of the gross payment – with a further reduction to 20 per cent of the gross payment (producing a fraction of 20/80ths) scheduled for 1994.

Capital Allowances and Investment Incentives

As already noted in Chapter 2, capital allowances differ in amount from the depreciation shown in a company's accounts. The main reason for this is that whereas a company in reporting to its shareholders is interested in calculating profit as fairly as possible, the government may also be interested in trying to encourage investment.

The method of calculating capital allowances has varied from time to time, as have the rates allowed. At the time of writing, most capital allowances are given in the form of annual writing-down allowances calculated on the reducing balance method, as illustrated in the depreciation example in Chapter 2 (p. 21). The rates vary according to the class of asset. There are no capital allowances on non-industrial buildings such as retail shops, offices and dwelling-houses.

It is important to note that all the allowances described above operate as deductions in the calculation of taxable income. If the latter is at least as large as the allowances, then the effect is to reduce the company's tax bill by the amount of the allowances multiplied by the corporation tax rate. A company which has no taxable income to offset against the allowances does not benefit at all.

This is not true of government grants. These are not reductions in taxable income but payments of cash to a company by the government. They are thus not dependent on the company making a taxable profit. The receipt of such grants does not affect capital allowances. It is standard accounting practice for grants relating to fixed assets to be credited to profit and loss account over the expected useful life of the asset, by treating the amount of the grant as a deferred credit (shown separately in the balance sheet), a portion of which is transferred to revenue annually. British Vita in 1992 credited government grants of £610,000 to profit and loss account [note 2, p. 27] and carried forward £1,107,000 as deferred income [p. 36]. Other grants are credited to revenue in the year in which the expenditure to which they relate is charged.

Deferred Taxation

Capital allowances greater than accounting depreciation ('accelerated capital allowances') are an example of what is known as a 'timing difference'. The effect is to reduce taxable income in the current year below the company's profit before tax.

It could be argued that the taxation payable has not been saved but merely 'deferred' to a later year. Whether, and if so how, a provision should be made for 'deferred taxation' is a matter which has aroused a lot of discussion in the accounting world. British Vita's policy in this matter is set out in its Accounting Policies [p. 26] as follows:

Deferred taxation is provided using the liability method in respect of timing differences except where the liability is not expected to arise in the foreseeable future. Advance corporation tax which is available to reduce the corporation tax payable on future profits is carried forward where recovery is reasonably assured and, to the extent appropriate, is deducted from the provision for deferred taxation.

British Vita thus, in accordance with standard accounting practice, makes provision not for all potential future deferred tax payable but only for that part where there is a reasonable probability that payment will have to be made in the foreseeable future (usually regarded as the next three years). Note 18 [pp. 37–8] discloses that 'full' provision for deferred tax would have amounted to £8,998,000, as distinct from the 'partial' provision made of £6,683,000.

The provision is smaller than it otherwise would have been by the amount of ACT recoverable deducted. ACT recoverable arises mainly because the ACT which British Vita has to pay on its proposed dividends is payable within the next accounting period (1993), whereas it is recoverable only in 1994. This gives rise to a *current* liability but not to a current asset. It is the asset amount which is deducted from the provision for deferred taxation.

Where a company has no liability to corporation tax, the ACT is not recoverable and has to be written off. Such a situation may be caused by a combination of low profitability and generous tax allowances.

Capital Gains Tax

Individuals are taxed not only on their income but also, at their top ('marginal') rate of income tax, on certain capital gains, that is, the excess of the price they receive on selling an asset over the price they paid for it. Individuals are entitled to an annual exempt amount on which the tax is not payable. Companies are not liable to capital gains tax on their capital gains, which are instead charged to corporation tax.

Tax does not become payable when an asset is revalued unless it is sold and even then the tax is postponed if a replacement is bought. Since fixed assets are held for use rather than sale, it is not the practice to make provision for the tax which would arise if the assets were sold for the revalued amount (see British Vita's note 18, p. 38).

If a gain is made from selling an asset owned on 6 April 1965, only that part of the gain related to the period from 6 April 1965 to the date of sale is taxable. It is for this reason that some companies include a note in their annual reports giving the market value of their shares at that date. (British Vita does not do so because it was not then a listed company.)

Close Companies

The Finance Act 1965 introduced the concept of the 'close company', defined as a company resident in the United Kingdom which is under the control of five or fewer participators and associates or of participators who are directors. The detailed legislation is extremely complex but has been of little practical importance since 1980. British Vita states in its Directors' Report that it is not a close company [p. 19].

Value Added Tax

Unlike the forms of taxation discussed so far, value added tax (VAT) is not a direct tax but an indirect tax, that is, one which is not assessed and collected from those intended to bear it. VAT is a multi-stage tax; manufacturing companies such as British Vita pay tax on their inputs, charge tax on their outputs and can set off the tax paid against the tax charged. Sales and purchases are included in the consolidated profit and loss account net of VAT, but trade debtors and trade creditors in the balance sheet include VAT.

Tax Law

The most important statutes (Acts of Parliament) relating to the taxes described in this chapter are the Income and Corporation Taxes Act 1988, the Capital Allowances Act 1990, the Taxation of Chargeable Gains Act 1992 and the Taxes Management Act 1970. Every year there is at least one Finance Act amending the law. There is also a large body of case law relating to taxation. The law is thus always changing and some of the statements made in this chapter will need modification as the years go by.

Audit Reports

As mentioned in the Directors' Responsibility Statement [p. 45], the preparation of the financial statements of a company and their presentation to the shareholders and to the tax authorities are the duties of the directors, not of the auditors, although the latter may give valuable assistance.

The Report of the Auditors to the members (i.e., shareholders) of British Vita Company Ltd [p. 45] reads as follows:

Auditors' report to the Members of British Vita PLC

We have audited the accounts on pages 22 to 44 in accordance with Auditing Standards.

In our opinion the accounts give a true and fair view of the state of affairs of the Company and the Group at 31 December 1992 and of the profit and cash flows of the Group and of the total recognised gains and losses of the Company and the Group for the year then ended and have been properly prepared in accordance with the Companies Act 1985.

The report is signed by Arthur Andersen and dated 9 March 1993, the same date on which the accounts were approved by the board of directors [p. 24]. Arthur Andersen are one of the 'Big Six' international accounting firms; the audits of UK listed companies are increasingly carried out by members of these firms. Arthur Andersen sign as 'Chartered Accountants and Registered Auditor'. This dual description recognizes firstly that the firm's partners are members of a major British professional accountancy body and secondly that the firm's name is inscribed on a statutory register as qualified for appointment as a company auditor. All three Institutes of Chartered Accountants (in England and Wales, of Scotland, in Ireland) provide, as does also the Chartered Association of Certified Accountants, a recognized professional qualification for company auditors, and keep registers.

The 1992 audit report follows the wording recommended at the time by the appropriate auditing standard. It is very brief and could be criticized as failing to supply sufficient information to shareholders and failing to inform readers whether their expectations of an audit were confirmed.

In 1993 it was replaced by a much longer report which reads as follows:

Auditors' Report to the Shareholders of XYZ PLC

We have audited the financial statements on pages . . . to . . . which have been prepared under the historical convention [as modified by the revaluation of certain fixed assets] and the accounting policies set out on page . . .

Respective responsibilities of directors and auditors
As described on page . . . the company's directors are responsible for the preparation of financial statements. It is our responsibility to form an independent opinion, based on our audit, on those statements and to report our opinion to you.

Basis of opinion

We conducted our audit in accordance with Auditing Standards issued by the Auditing Practices Board. An audit includes examination, on a test basis, of evidence relevant to the amounts and disclosures in the financial statements. It also includes an assessment of the significant estimates and judgements made by the directors in the preparation of the financial statements, and of whether the accounting policies are appropriate to the company's circumstances, consistently applied and adequately disclosed.

We planned and performed our audit so as to obtain all the information and explanations which we considered necessary in order to provide us with sufficient evidence to give reasonable assurance that the financial statements are free from material misstatement, whether caused by fraud or other irregularity or error. In forming our opinion we also evaluated the overall adequacy of the presentation of information in the financial statements.

Opinion

In our opinion the financial statements give a true and fair view of the state of the company's affairs as at 31 December 19 .. and of its profit [loss] for the year then ended and have been properly prepared in accordance with the Companies Act 1985.

There are a number of interesting points to note about this report:

1. It is a report, not a certificate or guarantee: the auditors report their opinion; they do not certify or guarantee anything.
2. What they give their opinion on is compliance with the Companies Act and the 'truth and fairness' of the accounts. This is not the same as saying that the accounts are 'correct' or 'right' in every particular. It should be clear from the discussion of the financial statements in Chapter 2 that the figures in balance sheets and profit and loss accounts are necessarily based to a certain extent on estimates and judgements made by the directors.
3. Reference is made to the basis on which the financial statements have been prepared. In the UK this is normally the historical cost convention, often modified by the revaluation of fixed assets. As will be seen in Chapter 4, a few UK companies follow the current cost convention.
4. The auditors are reporting to the shareholders of British Vita, not to the directors. Their function, as a late-nineteenth-century

English judge put it, is to serve as a 'watchdog' for the share-holders. They are appointed by the shareholders, usually on the recommendation of the directors. Appointment is made each year by resolution at the annual general meeting.

5. The auditors do not report on whether or not frauds have been committed but limit themselves to stating that they have sought reasonable assurance that the financial statements are free of material misstatements caused by fraud.
6. A careful distinction is made between the respective responsibilities of the directors and the auditors.
7. A brief description is given of the way in which an audit is carried out, with a reference to the auditing standards issued by the Auditing Practices Board (APB).

The report set out above is suitable when the auditors give an unqualified opinion. Occasionally auditors give a qualified opinion or are even unable to form an opinion (known as 'disclaimer of opinion'). Qualified opinions may arise if there is a limitation on the scope of the auditors' examination or the auditors are in disagreement with the directors on the treatment or disclosure of a matter in the financial statements.

Audit Expectations Gap

The wording of UK audit reports is an amalgam of legal requirements and of what the accountancy profession considers to be the function of the audit. This does not necessarily coincide with what all users of audit reports would prefer and in recent years there has emerged what is known as the 'audit expectations gap'.

A discussion document, *Auditing into the Twenty-first Century*, issued by the Research Committee of the Institute of Chartered Accountants of Scotland in 1993 identified these public expectations as follows:

(1) the financial statements are right;
(2) the company will not fail;
(3) there has been no fraud;

    (4) the company has acted within the law;

    (5) the company has been competently managed;

    (6) the company has adopted a responsible attitude to environmental and societal matters;

    (7) the external auditors are independent of the directors;

    (8) the external auditors will report to a third party if they suspect that the directors are involved in fraud or other illegal activity;

    (9) the external auditors are accountable to a wide range of stakeholders;

  (10) the external auditors are financially liable if they fail in any of their duties.

Some of these expectations are already being met in full or in part, but neither the government nor the accountancy profession is likely to accept that all of them are reasonable, in the sense that there is an effective demand for them and there are auditors capable of supplying them at a reasonable cost.

We have already seen that no financial statements can be regarded as 'right' as distinct from 'true and fair'. Auditors are likely to continue to report on the latter. Neither the directors nor its auditors can guarantee that a company will not fail but there is a growing consensus that directors can reasonably be expected to state, and auditors to report on, whether or not a company is likely to remain a going concern for the ensuing twelve months. Auditors cannot guarantee that there has been no material fraud but they can report whether or not there are systems of internal control which minimize opportunities for fraud and maximize the likelihood that any such fraud will be quickly detected. Similarly, while auditors cannot guarantee that a company has in all respects acted within the law, they can confirm that there are internal control systems which minimize the opportunities for committing illegal acts and maximize the likelihood of speedy detection.

On the other hand, auditors, as experts in accounting and finance, are not necessarily qualified to assess the competence of management or to report on environmental and societal matters, although these could well be the subject of a separate 'environmental audit'.

It is obviously important that auditors should not only be skilled in their profession but also be, and be seen to be, independent of the directors and managers of the company being audited. Company law already requires that an auditor must not be an officer or servant of the company or of any company in the group, or a partner or employee of such officer or servant. The amount of the auditors' remuneration must be stated in the annual report. For the British Vita group in 1992 it was £769,000 [note 2, p. 27]. Auditors may (and commonly do) also provide other services (e.g., taxation advice) to companies, although some commentators argue that this may endanger their independence. The amount received for any such services must be separately disclosed. For the British Vita group in 1992 it was £28,000 [note 2, p. 27]. Like many listed companies British Vita has established an audit committee composed of non-executives. Its function is to review the half year and annual financial statements and matters related to both external audit and internal audit [p. 18].

Auditors of financial institutions are already required to report to a regulatory body when they are satisfied that it is necessary to do so in order to protect the interests of shareholders or depositors. It is possible that, despite the problems of confidentiality, this obligation may be extended to other types of companies.

As already noted, the external auditors are accountable to, and report to, the shareholders, although their report is also in practice relied upon by other stakeholders in the company. It can be argued, therefore, that auditors ought to be legally liable to other stakeholders as well. The House of Lords has recently upheld, however, in the Caparo case (1990) that auditors owe a duty of care to the shareholders as a whole, not to individual shareholders or to other persons. This decision has been much criticized.

4. Regulation, Formats, Accounting Standards and Inflation

Regulation

In order to draw up a set of financial statements for a company it is necessary to make decisions about:

(1) what should be disclosed (*disclosure*);
(2) the format of the statements (*presentation*);
(3) the rules of measurement and valuation (*measurement*).

Who should make these decisions; that is, how, if at all, should company financial statements be regulated? There are a number of possibilities:

(1) Each company is allowed to decide for itself.
(2) A private-sector body composed wholly, mainly or partly of accountants, as acknowledged experts in the field, makes the decisions.
(3) The government makes the decisions by means of, for example:
(i) legislation;
(ii) a government-appointed regulatory body;
(iii) a national accounting plan;
(iv) an accounting court.

It is possible, of course, that a mixture of the above methods may be appropriate.

Whichever methods are chosen, there are costs and benefits. No one method is likely to be ideal for all countries and at all times. In this chapter we shall look at the British approach in the 1990s. It has to be remembered that it is the result of a century and a half of evolution and that British ideas on the subject are strongly influenced by the United States and by the other member states of the EC.

During the nineteenth century most British companies were allowed complete freedom in matters of disclosure, presentation and measurement. During the first half of the twentieth century it gradually became accepted that, while the government should not interfere with presentation and measurement, it ought to prescribe by legislation what should be disclosed. This was the general philosophy behind the Companies Act 1948. The Act imposed two obligations on company directors: firstly, to prepare balance sheets and profit and loss accounts which gave a 'true and fair view' and, secondly, to give the detailed information specified in a Schedule to the Act. No definition was given of the phrase 'true and fair'.

This approach was commented on favourably in the report of the 1962 committee on company law amendment:

In our view the general scheme of the Act in this respect is the right one, namely to indicate in general terms the objectives and the standard of disclosure required and also to prescribe certain specific information that must be given. The formula 'true and fair' seems to us satisfactory as an indication of the required standard, while it makes for certainty to prescribe certain specific information which the law regards as the minimum necessary for the purpose of attaining that standard.
(*Report of the Company Law Committee*, Cmnd 1749, HMSO, 1962, para. 332)

The committee went on to state that 'it is primarily to the initiative of the professional associations that we must look if the general principles of the Act are to be effectively applied in practice' (para. 334). They referred in particular to the Recommendations on Accounting Principles issued periodically by the Institute of Chartered Accountants in England and Wales. It was through these Recommendations (issued between 1942 and 1969) that the professional accountancy bodies began to involve themselves in matters of disclosure and measurement.

During the 1960s the quality of published financial statements was increasingly criticized. The profession, encouraged by the government, responded in 1970 with the establishment of an Accounting Standards Committee (ASC). The ASC was replaced in 1990 by the Accounting Standards Board (ASB) (see below).

The British government has made no serious attempt to control company financial statements through a regulatory agency (as exists in the United States in the form of the Securities and Exchange Commission) or a national accounting plan (as in France). It has, however, intervened on matters of disclosure and in the debate about inflation accounting (see below) and, as a result of Britain's entry into the European Community, has legislated on presentation and measurement.

In Britain, then, it is company legislation and accounting standards which largely determine what goes into published financial statements. Less important influences are tax legislation and the requirements of the Stock Exchange. Tax legislation influences published accounts because companies may find it inconvenient to follow one set of practices for tax purposes and another for reporting to shareholders. Accounting practices banned for tax calculations tend to be unpopular in published financial statements, but there is no compulsion for a company to follow tax rules in those statements. (In this respect Britain differs from many continental European countries.) Stock Exchange requirements for listed companies do not go much beyond those of company law and accounting standards.

The detailed requirements of the Companies Act 1985, as amended in 1989, are summarized in the Glossary (Appendix B) under a number of headings, the most important of which are: Debtors, Directors' Emoluments, Directors' Report, Distributable Reserves, Employee Information, Liabilities, Segment Reporting, True and Fair View, Turnover and Undistributable Reserves.

Formats

Companies have a choice of two balance sheet formats and four profit and loss account formats. The minimum requirements of one of the balance sheet formats are illustrated in Table 4.1. The other format is very similar except that it is set out horizontally rather

Table 4.1. Balance Sheet Format

Fixed assets			
Intangible assets	×		
Tangible assets	×		
Investments	×		
			×
Current assets			
Stocks	×		
Debtors	×		
Investments	×		
Cash at bank and in hand	×	×	
Creditors: amounts falling due within one year		×	
Net current assets (liabilities)			×
Total assets less current liabilities			× ×
Creditors: amounts falling due after more than one year			×
Provisions for liabilities and charges			×
Capital and reserves			
Called up share capital	×		
Share premium account	×		
Revaluation reserve	×		
Other reserves	×		
Profit and loss account	×		×
Minority interests			×
			× ×

than vertically. Headings for which there is no balance may be omitted, and additional detail may be added. British Vita, for example, has omitted the heading 'Intangible assets'.

The four profit and loss account formats are more flexible. Two are vertical and two horizontal. Most companies publish a profit and loss account very much like British Vita's, but others disclose the costs of raw materials and consumables, staff costs and depreciation, instead of cost of sales, distribution costs and administrative expenses.

The directors of small companies (defined in terms of total assets, turnover and average number of employees) have the privilege of preparing and filing abbreviated accounts if they so wish. Medium-sized companies are also granted some exemptions in what they can file with the Registrar of Companies, but the abbreviations do not in their case apply to the financial statements sent to shareholders. Subsidiaries may use the abbreviations only if the group to which they belong is as a whole small or medium. No public companies may be regarded as small or medium. Small and medium *groups* are exempted from filing consolidated accounts with the Registrar.

Summary Financial Statements

The cost of sending out a full set of financial statements to all shareholders is quite considerable, especially for companies such as British Gas, which, as noted in Chapter 1, has over two million shareholders. It is probably for this reason that listed companies are permitted to issue financial statements which summarize the information contained in the annual accounts and directors' report. The issue of summary financial statements is optional (British Vita does not issue them, for example) and shareholders who state that they wish to receive the full accounts must be sent them. The form of summary financial investments is prescribed by regulation and comprises the main items from the directors' report, consolidated profit and loss account, and balance sheet. Summary financial statements are not necessarily simpler to understand than a full set of statements.

Accounting Standards

The Accounting Standards Board is prescribed under company law as an accounting standards setting body. The Companies Act requires companies (other than small and medium companies) to state whether their accounts have been prepared in accordance with 'applicable accounting standards' and to give particulars of any material departure from those standards and the reasons for them. The ASB issues Financial Reporting Standards (FRSs) and has also adopted the extant Statements of Standard Accounting Practice

(SSAPs) issued by the ASC. SSAPs are gradually being replaced by FRSs.

The ASB has nine members appointed by the Financial Reporting Council. The chairman and the technical director are full time, the other members part time. (The ASC had more than twice as many members but all were part time.) The members of the ASB are drawn from the accountancy profession, commerce, industry, the City of London and the public sector. Unlike the former ASC, the ASB is independent of the member bodies of the Consultative Committee of Accountancy Bodies (the Institute of Chartered Accountants in England and Wales, the Institute of Chartered Accountants of Scotland, the Institute of Chartered Accountants in Ireland, the Chartered Association of Certified Accountants, the Chartered Institute of Management Accountants and the Chartered Institute of Public Finance and Accountancy) and issues accounting standards on its own authority. However, it only issues an FRS after extensive consultation, which always includes an 'exposure draft' for comment by interested parties.

As at 31 December 1993, four FRSs had been issued and nineteen SSAPs were still extant:

FRSs

1. Cash flow statements
2. Accounting for subsidiary companies
3. Reporting financial performance
4. Capital instruments

SSAPs

1. Accounting for the results of associated companies
2. Disclosure of accounting policies
3. Earnings per share
4. The accounting treatment of government grants
5. Accounting for value added tax
8. The treatment of taxation under the imputation system in the accounts of companies
9. Stocks and work in progress
12. Accounting for depreciation
13. Accounting for research and development

15. Accounting for deferred taxation
17. Accounting for post balance sheet events
18. Accounting for contingencies
19. Accounting for investment properties
20. Foreign currency translation
21. Accounting for leases and hire purchase contracts
22. Accounting for goodwill
23. Accounting for acquisitions and mergers
24. Accounting for pension costs
25. Segmental reporting

The ASC also approved the issue of non-mandatory Statements of Recommended Practice (SORPs). The ASC prepared and issued SORPs on pension scheme accounts and accounting by charities. SORPs have also been issued by other bodies, such as the Oil Industry Accounting Committee, and approved by the ASC. The ASB does not issue or approve ('frank') SORPs but may issue, if appropriate, a negative assurance statement.

One reason for the replacement of the ASC by the ASB was the difficulty that the former had in persuading companies to comply with accounting standards issued by professional accountancy bodies with no legal right to lay down measurement rules or to say what must be disclosed in company financial statements. The ASB's standards, unlike those of the ASC, have the recognition of law. In addition, a Financial Reporting Review Panel was set up in 1991 under the Companies Act. The main task of the panel is to examine material departures from company law and accounting standards by companies. The panel is empowered to apply to the court for a declaration that the accounts of a company do not comply with the requirements of the Act and for an order requiring the company's directors to prepare revised accounts. In practice, companies have so far always agreed to rectify their accounts without the intervention of the court. The panel is not an 'accounting court' of the style that exists in the Netherlands but in both that country and the UK the courts are used to improve compliance with accounting standards.

FRSs and SSAPs are very important and references to them will be found throughout this book. The ways in which accounting standards are set or should be set have been much discussed. To some extent standard setting is inevitably a 'political' process since standard setting bodies, to be effective, must take account of the (sometimes conflicting) interests of the users and preparers of financial statements. Standard setters may wish, however, to take account as far as possible of a conceptual framework, a set of interrelated concepts underlying the procedures of financial accounting. Explicit conceptual frameworks have been drawn up in the United States and Australia and also by the International Accounting Standards Committee (of which the UK professional accountancy bodies are members). The ASB has issued a draft of its *Statement of Principles for Financial Reporting*.

The most general accounting standard is SSAP 2 on the disclosure of accounting policies. This sets out four basic assumptions or concepts which are said to underlie the periodic accounts of business enterprises:

1. The 'going concern' concept: the enterprise will continue in operational existence for the foreseeable future.
2. The 'accruals' concept: revenues and costs are accrued (that is, recognized as they are earned or incurred, not as money is received or paid), matched with one another as far as their relationship can be established or justifiably assumed, and dealt with in the profit and loss account of the period to which they relate.
3. The 'consistency' concept: there is consistency of accounting treatment of like items within each accounting period and from one period to the next.
4. The 'prudence' concept: revenue and profits are not anticipated, but are recognized by inclusion in the profit and loss account only when realized in the form either of cash or of other assets the ultimate realization of which can be assessed with reasonable certainty; provision is made for all known liabilities whether the amount of these is known with certainty or is a best estimate in the light of the information available.

Most accountants would agree that the above concepts are reasonably descriptive of actual practice; not all would accept that these are the concepts which *ought* to be followed. In particular, there are those who think too much stress is laid on prudence, or conservatism as they would prefer to call it.

Concepts not mentioned in SSAP 2 are 'objectivity' and 'substance over form'. Objectivity refers to the need to establish rules for recording financial transactions and events which as far as possible do not depend on the personal judgement of the recorder. This has led to a bias in favour of using the cost of acquisition, or historical cost as it is usually called. A brief description of traditional British accounting practice would be historical cost modified by prudence. Many accountants have denied that it is a function of a balance sheet to show how much a company is worth. It is, they have argued, merely a historical record. Other accountants have argued, however, that a balance sheet which did not attempt to show how much a company is worth would be of little use to the shareholders.

'Substance over form' is a concept whereby transactions or other events are accounted for and presented in accordance with what is perceived to be their economic reality rather than their legal 'form'. It is particularly applicable to borrowings which are not legally debt and therefore might be shown 'off balance sheet' but which have the same economic function as debt. Finance leases (see Chapter 8), for example, fall into this category.

As a result of SSAP 2, companies publish statements of 'accounting policies' setting out the way in which they have dealt with a number of matters. British Vita's statement, for example [p. 26], covers the basis of the accounts (that is, the historical cost convention modified to include the revaluation of certain fixed assets), the basis of consolidation, foreign currency stocks, turnover, leases, depreciation of tangible fixed assets, grants, research and development, patents and trade marks, pensions and deferred taxation.

Accounting for Inflation

During the last two decades changes in both general and specific prices and fluctuating exchange rates have caused many problems for accountants. Table 4.2 shows the fall in the domestic purchasing

Table 4.2. Inflation Rates, 1971–92

	Index (average for calendar year)	Percentage increase over the previous year
1971	20.3	—
1972	21.7	6.9
1973	23.7	9.2
1974	27.5	16.0
1975	34.2	24.4
1976	39.8	16.4
1977	46.1	15.8
1978	50.0	8.5
1979	56.7	13.4
1980	66.8	17.8
1981	74.8	12.0
1982	81.2	8.6
1983	84.9	4.6
1984	89.2	5.1
1985	94.6	6.1
1986	97.8	3.4
1987	101.9	4.2
1988	106.9	4.9
1989	115.2	7.8
1990	126.1	9.5
1991	133.5	5.9
1992	138.5	3.7

Source. Index of Retail Prices (1 January 1987 = 100) as reported in *Accountancy*.

power of the 'pound in the pocket'. Table 4.3 shows the fluctuations of the pound sterling in relation to the United States dollar.

The Companies Act distinguishes between 'historical cost accounting rules' which require the application to financial statements of conventional accounting procedures based on historical cost modified by prudence, and 'alternative accounting rules' which permit not only the use of current cost valuations but also a mixture of historical and current valuations. British Vita, like many other companies, prepares its financial statements 'under the historical cost convention modified to include the revaluation of certain fixed assets' [p. 26].

In times of inflation, balance sheet values based on historical cost

Table 4.3. The Rate of Exchange of £1 to US$1, 1971–92

31 December 1971	2.55
1972	2.35
1973	2.32
1974	2.35
1975	2.02
1976	1.70
1977	1.91
1978	2.03
1979	2.22
1980	2.38
1981	1.91
1982	1.62
1983	1.45
1984	1.16
1985	1.45
1986	1.47
1987	1.87
1988	1.81
1989	1.61
1990	1.93
1991	1.87
1992	1.51

Source. UN Monthly Bulletin of Statistics.

rapidly become divorced from current market values, and objectivity and prudence can lead paradoxically to an overstatement of profits. This is most easily understood in relation to fixed assets and depreciation. If fixed assets are valued at historical cost, depreciation will usually be based on historical cost as well. This will result in a lower depreciation charge, and hence a higher profit, than if both the asset and the depreciation were written up to, say, current replacement cost. It can reasonably be argued that the use of historical costs during a period of inflation can lead to the publication of profit figures which are in part fictitious. The distribution of such profits would mean a running down of the *real* (as opposed to the money) capital of the company.

The attempts by the leaders of the accountancy profession to introduce some form of inflation accounting have been beset by many difficulties.★

Two principal methods of accounting for inflation have been debated. As noted below, neither of these is much used in practice.

1. Adjustments for changes in the *general* price level only, that is, current purchasing power (CPP) accounting.
2. Adjustments for changes in *specific* prices, that is current cost accounting (CCA).

The two methods differ in their approach to profit measurement and asset valuation. CPP accounting values assets in terms of the current purchasing power of the sums of money originally invested. While under historical cost accounting no profit is deemed to be earned unless the original money capital invested is maintained intact, under CPP accounting it is the purchasing power of that capital that has to be maintained. In practice, CPP accounting means that non-monetary assets (that is, fixed assets and stocks) are valued at historical cost adjusted by a general price index (e.g., the retail price index). All profit and loss account items are restated by the same index. In addition, profit is decreased or increased by a purchasing power loss or gain calculated on the company's net monetary assets during the period.

The CCA method, on the other hand, values assets at their 'value to the business', that is, the lower of current replacement cost and 'recoverable amount', the latter being the higher of an asset's net realizable value and the amount recoverable from its further use in the business. In the profit and loss account, current revenues are matched with current costs and no profit is deemed to be earned unless the company has maintained its physical capacity. In practice, CCA profit is calculated by making four adjustments to historical cost operating profit. The adjustments are:

(1) a cost of sales adjustment (COSA);
(2) a monetary working capital adjustment (MWCA);
(3) a depreciation adjustment;
(4) a gearing adjustment.

* For a lively account by a participant, see C. A. Westwick, 'The Lessons to be Learned from the Development of Inflation Accounting in the UK', *Accounting and Business Research*, Autumn 1980.

The adjustments are applied in two stages:

1. To arrive at the *current cost operating profit*. This is equal to the historical cost operating profit after deduction of the first three adjustments. It represents the surplus arising from the ordinary activities of the business, after allowing for the impact of price changes on the funds needed to continue the existing business and to maintain its operating capability, but without taking into account the way in which it is financed. It is calculated before interest and before taxation.
2. To arrive at the *current cost profit attributable to shareholders*. This is the current cost operating profit after deduction of the gearing adjustment. It represents the surplus for the period after allowing for the impact of price changes on the funds needed to maintain the shareholders' proportion of the operating capabilities of the group.

The cost of sales adjustment is made in order to base the cost of sales on the cost current at the time of consumption instead of the time of purchase. This can be done in various ways – for example, by the use of appropriate specific price indices and the so-called averaging method (that is, the adjustment is equal to the average *physical* stock multiplied by the price increase during the year).

Increased prices tie up in the business not only more stocks but also more monetary working capital (that is, in essence, bank balances + debtors – creditors). The MWCA can be calculated by the averaging method in a similar way to the COSA. The depreciation adjustment is made in order to base depreciation on current replacement cost instead of historical cost.

The gearing adjustment is the most controversial. It is intended to indicate the benefit to shareholders of the use of long-term debt, measured by the extent to which the net operating assets are financed by borrowing. In effect, as calculated in SSAP 16, it reduces the three current cost adjustments by the proportion which has been financed by borrowing. The concept of 'gearing' is discussed further in Chapter 8.

The ASC originally preferred CPP accounting, and this was the basis of the provisional SSAP 7 issued in 1974. The government-appointed Sandilands Committee, however, which reported in 1975, rejected CPP accounting in favour of CCA. The standard finally accepted in 1980, SSAP 16, was CCA based. However, lower rates of inflation and controversy about the details of the standard made SSAP 16 difficult to enforce, and it is no longer mandatory. Like most companies, British Vita provides no CCA data in its 1992 annual report. Only a few listed UK companies, most of them public utilities, provide such data. One example is British Gas.

Accounting for Foreign Exchange

British Vita's subsidiaries and associated companies outside the UK normally keep their accounts in the appropriate local currency. These foreign financial statements are translated using year-end rates of exchange, that is, by the 'closing rate' method. This is the method that standard accounting practice requires for subsidiaries which operate as separate or quasi-independent entities. Companies can choose under this method to translate *profit and loss account* items at either the closing rate or the average rate for the year. In 1992, British Vita adopted the former method but in 1993, as stated in its Interim Report, it changed to average rates.

If the rates at the end of the period differ from those obtaining at the beginning of the year, an exchange or translation difference will arise. Under the closing rate method such gains or losses are dealt with through reserves and do not affect the profit for the financial year. In a world of sharply fluctuating exchange rates, exchange differences can be quite large. British Vita in 1992 recorded positive exchange rate differences of £15,405,000 [note 20, p. 39] equal to 46 per cent of its profit for the financial year of £33,545,000.

An alternative method of foreign currency translation is the so-called 'temporal method', which is used where the operations of the foreign entity are regarded as an integral part of those of the parent company. The temporal method differs from the closing rate method in that those assets recorded in the local currency at historical cost rather than at a current value (that is, fixed assets and most stocks) are translated at the rates ruling at the dates of acquisition. Also, and very importantly, exchange gains and losses are passed through the profit and loss account. Under the temporal method, groups whose parent company's currency is strengthening tend to show translation gains, while those whose parent company's currency is weakening tend to show translation losses.

For foreign entities whose economies are experiencing very high rates of inflation ('hyper-inflation'), British standard accounting practice requires before application of the closing rate method either restatement of the financial statements to take account of local inflation or for the subsidiary to keep its accounts in an appropriate non-local currency (e.g., US dollars).

Foreign exchange *transactions* are translated into sterling at the appropriate forward contract or rate of exchange at the date of the transaction.

Creative Accounting

Financial statements can be used to mislead users as well as to inform them. Such 'creative accounting' became more common in the UK in the 1980s, intensifying the conflict between legal form and economic substance. Creative accounting usually involves emphasizing the letter of accounting rules rather than their spirit. The overriding requirement to give a true and fair view should be able to prevent this but it has not always succeeded in doing so in practice. Much ingenuity has been devoted to maximizing earnings per share, improving liquidity by window-dressing and minimizing gearing ratios. There is discussion of each of these in Chapters 7 and 8.

5. Tools of Analysis and Sources of Information

> . . . high Heaven rejects the lore
> Of nicely-calculated less or more.
>
> William Wordsworth,
> 'Inside of King's College Chapel, Cambridge'

The first four chapters of this book have been mainly descriptive. In the chapters which follow we turn to analysis and interpretation. We shall be concerned with three main questions:

1. Is the company under analysis making a satisfactory profit?
2. Is the company likely to run out of cash, or to keep cash idle?
3. How does the company decide the sources of its long-term funds?

These are the related problems of profitability, liquidity and capital structure.

Our tools of analysis will be the relationships which exist among the different items in the financial statements ('financial ratios') and the rates of return linking outflows with expected inflows ('yields').

Financial Ratios

Financial ratios are normally expressed either as percentages or by the number of times one figure can be divided into another. For example, if a company has current assets of £10,000 and current liabilities of £5,000, we could say that current liabilities are 50 per cent of current assets, that current assets are 200 per cent of current liabilities, that the ratio $\frac{\text{current assets}}{\text{current liabilities}}$ is 2.0 or that the ratio

$\dfrac{\text{current liabilities}}{\text{current assets}}$ is 0.5. Which method is chosen is a matter of convenience and convention. In the example quoted it is customary to speak of a current ratio, $\dfrac{\text{current assets}}{\text{current liabilities}}$, of 2.0. (A percentage, as can be seen from the above, is merely a ratio multiplied by 100.)

Not all ratios and percentages are significant or useful, and one must guard against the temptation to calculate them for their own sake. The component parts of a ratio must be reasonably related to each other and measure something important. It is unlikely, for example, that much can be gained from a scrutiny of the relationship between current liabilities and goodwill. The limitations of conventional historical cost accounting must always be kept in mind, and accounting figures should not be treated as more precise than they really are. There is little sense in calculating a ratio to more than two decimal places.

A single ratio in isolation seldom provides much information. Each ratio calculated should either provide additional confirmation of what has already been deduced or act as a guide to the further questions which need to be asked.

Yields

A yield is a rate of return relating outflows to inflows. If, for example, I buy for £50 an irredeemable government bond with a par value of £100 on which interest of 4 per cent is payable annually, there is an immediate cash outflow of £50, followed by a series of cash inflows of £4 each year in perpetuity. The yield (gross of tax) is $\dfrac{4 \times 100}{50}$ per cent, (i.e., 8 per cent). If the bond were redeemable at a fixed price at some date in the future, there would be a difference between the flat yield, which takes only the interest into account, and the redemption yield, which takes the redemption price into account as well. For example, if the bond is redeemable twenty years hence at par, the flat yield is about 5.0 per cent and the redemption yield about 9.8 per cent.

The Need for Comparisons

As already noted, any ratio, percentage or yield is of little value in isolation. It is necessary to have some standard with which to compare it. The standard can be a budgeted one, set by the company for itself; a historical one, based on the past performance of the company; or an industry one, based on the observed ratios of companies in the same industry.

Budgeted standards are not usually available to shareholders or external financial analysts. Historical comparisons are often given in annual reports: see, for example, pp. 4–5 of British Vita's report, headed 'Summary of Financial Data 1988–1992'. This presents information in the form not only of raw data (e.g., turnover, operating profit) and ratios (e.g., operating profit as a percentage of turnover) but also in the form of pie charts (turnover by class of business and by geographical destination) and graphs (e.g., a time series of earnings per share and dividends).

Industry Ratios

Industry ratios pose a much more difficult problem to the financial analyst. There are a number of reasons for this.

Firstly, it is often difficult to decide to which industry a company belongs. Many industries are, in fact, composed of a surprisingly heterogeneous group of companies. In the Stock Exchange industrial classification at the date on which its 1992 Annual Report was published British Vita is included in the plastics and rubber fabricators' group, which includes nine other companies. British Vita is the largest of the ten companies, with almost half of the total industry turnover. It is the only company in the industry with substantial overseas sales. (The standard industrial classification used in government publications is not identical with the Stock Exchange classification and both are revised from time to time. In this book we shall follow the custom of most financial analysts in using the latter.)

Secondly, the emphasis of the system of accounting at present in use is more on *consistency* for a particular company over time, than on *comparability* among different companies at a single point in time, and the analyst must constantly be on his guard against differences in definition and in methods of measurement.

Thirdly, companies end their accounting periods on different dates, so that industry ratios are perforce averages of ratios calculated at different dates and for different periods.

For these reasons not too much reliance can be placed on an industry comparison which is based on ratios obtained from published accounts. Companies can, however, obtain comparable ratios by taking part in a properly conducted comparison, such as those conducted by the Centre for Interfirm Comparison.* But such ratios are, by their very nature, confidential and unavailable to the external analyst. Individual and industry ratios are, however, available on a commercial basis from a number of sources, including Dun & Bradstreet, Extel and Datastream.

Sources of Information

In this section are listed a number of useful sources of information relating to individual companies, to industries or to the company sector as a whole. The list is not intended to be exhaustive. Most of the items should be available in a good public or university library. The Government Statistical Service publishes each year a brief, up-to-date guide to government statistics (*Government Statistics: A Brief Guide to Sources*). There is also a more comprehensive *Guide to Official Statistics*.

1. *The Times 1000* (published annually by *The Times*). This lists each year, among other things, the thousand largest British industrial companies (ranked by turnover), with details of their turnover; capital employed (defined as total tangible assets less current liabilities, other than bank loans and overdrafts and future tax); net profit before interest and tax; net profit before interest and tax as a percentage of turnover; net profit before

---

* See H. Ingham and L. T. Harrington, *Interfirm Comparison*, Heinemann, 1980.

interest and tax as a percentage of capital employed; number of employees; and the market capitalization of the equity (that is, the total market value of all the company's ordinary shares). British Vita is in the top 200 of the thousand.

2. *Financial Statistics* (published monthly by the Government Statistical Service; an 'explanatory handbook' is published annually). Section 8 provides data about companies.
3. *British Business* (published weekly by the Department of Trade and Industry).
4. *Economic Trends* (published monthly by the Government Statistical Service).
5. *Bank of England Quarterly Bulletin.*
6. *United Kingdom National Accounts* (the 'CSO Blue Book'; published annually by the Government Statistical Service).

Statistics on the company sector are published from time to time in numbers 3 to 6. The first three also carry useful articles interpreting the statistics.

7. *Stock Exchange Quarterly* (published by the London Stock Exchange).
8. *Quality of Markets Companies Book* (published annually by the London Stock Exchange).
9. *Stock Exchange Official Yearbook* (published annually by Macmillan for the London Stock Exchange).

These last three publications provide a wealth of information on all aspects of the UK stock market.

10. *Financial Reporting. A Survey of Published Accounts* (published annually by the Institute of Chartered Accountants in England and Wales). This is a guide to current accounting requirements and an analysis of methods and examples of financial reporting used by 300 major British industrial and commercial companies.
11. *Accounting Standards* (published annually by the Institute of Chartered Accountants in England and Wales). This contains the full texts of all UK exposure drafts and accounting standards extant at 1 May each year. It also contains background material on the Accounting Standards Board.

12. *Sources of British Business Comparative Performance Data* (2nd edn, 1986, no. 193 in the Accountants Digest Series published by the Institute of Chartered Accountants in England and Wales).

6. Profitability, Return on Investment and Value Added

For what is Worth in anything
But so much Money as 'twill bring.

Samuel Butler,
Hudibras, I, i

Profitability

One of the first questions a shareholder is likely to ask of his company is whether it is making a profit. If so, is it making a satisfactory profit? We have already encountered some of the difficulties which arise in trying to measure profit. Although accountants try to make measurements as objective as possible, many financial numbers, even those purporting to represent past events, are necessarily to some extent estimates. Profit calculations are especially affected by the difficulties of measuring depreciation and valuing stock-in-trade, difficulties which are accentuated in times of changing price levels.

Return on Investment

Sales (turnover) and profits should not be looked at in isolation from the investment in net assets made to achieve them. The relationship between them can be set out as follows:

$$\text{Return on investment (ROI)} = \frac{\text{profit}}{\text{net assets}} = \frac{\text{profit}}{\text{sales}} \times \frac{\text{sales}}{\text{net assets}}$$

As already noted, there are a number of 'profit' figures in British Vita's consolidated profit and loss account, namely, gross profit, operating profit, profit on ordinary activities before interest, profit on ordinary activities before taxation, profit on ordinary activities after taxation, profit for the financial year and retained profit for the financial year. Only two of these profit measurers are suitable for use in the present context. They are (a) operating profit and (b) profit on ordinary activities before interest (which is equal to operating profit plus share of profit of associated undertakings). The strength of these measures is that, while taking account (as gross profit does not) of most of the revenues and expenses, they are not affected by interest on loans, dividends on shares, taxation or extraordinary items. If return on investment is to be a satisfactory measure of managerial performance on a continuing basis, it should not be influenced by changes in financial structure (see Chapter 8) or by changes in rates of tax. Similarly, it should not be affected by extraordinary items. The advantage of (a) over (b) is that it produces a return on investment measure which is easier to decompose since it does not include the profits of associated undertakings and can therefore be compared with turnover figures which, as we have seen (p. 28), do not include sales made by such companies.

If 'profit' is defined as operating profit or profit before interest, 'net assets' must be defined consistently as total assets less current liabilities (but not long-term liabilities) using either averages or end-of-year figures. Total assets less current liabilities can also be called 'capital employed'. It is equal in amount to shareholders' funds plus long-term liabilities.

In principle, return on investment can be measured in either historical cost or current cost terms. In practice, most companies (British Vita among them) provide only historical cost data, although these are often modified by the revaluation of land and buildings.

All the relevant figures for British Vita for 1988–1992 are set out on pp. 4–5 of its 1992 Annual Report. Details of the necessary calculations are given in Tables 6.1 and 6.2.

The tables show a steady increase in turnover and net assets over the five years, turnover increasing by 71 per cent from £508,676,000 in 1988 to £872,173,000 in 1992, and net assets increasing by 110

Table 6.1. Calculation of Return on Investment, British Vita Group, 1989–92

	Operating profit (a) £'000	Share of profit of associated undertakings (b) £'000	Profit on ordinary activities before interest and taxation (c) = (a) + (b) £'000	Net assets (total assets less current liabilities) (d) £'000	Average net assets (e)[1] £'000	Profit on ordinary activities before interest and taxation as a percentage of average net assets (f) = (c)/(e) × 100 %
1988	33,588	4,094	37,682	161,285	—	—
1989	43,454	5,353	48,807	192,293	176,789	27.6
1990	56,408	4,468	60,876	211,929	202,111	30.1
1991	53,338	1,624	54,962	222,452	217,191	25.3
1992	48,691	5,623	54,314	338,277	280,365	19.4

[1] Average net assets for 1992 is equal to the average of net assets 1991 and net assets 1992, and similarly for other years.

Source: British Vita PLC, Annual Report and Accounts 1992, pp. 4–5.

Table 6.2. Calculation of Operating Profit as Percentage of Turnover, British Vita Group, 1988–92

	Turnover (a) £000	Operating profit (b) £000	Operating profit as a percentage of turnover (c) = (b)/(a) × 100 %
1988	508,676	33,588	6.6
1989	655,837	43,454	6.6
1990	721,364	56,408	7.8
1991	770,166	53,338	6.9
1992	872,173	48,691	5.6

Source. ibid, p. 4.

per cent from £161,285,000 to £338,277,000. The group did not increase in profitability and return on investment to the same extent, the increases in the return on investment and operating profit to turnover percentages both being reversed in the difficult years of 1991 and 1992.

Nevertheless, as the figures on p. 4 of the Report show, profit on ordinary activities before taxation increased in 1992 after falling in 1991. This is explained by the interest receivable and payable figures detailed in note 4 [p. 28] and in the cash flow statement [p. 25]. Interest receivable increased and interest payable decreased, probably due in part to the rights issue made during 1992 which brought more investable cash into the company and allowed loans to be repaid.

Analysing the Profit and Loss Account

The detail provided in the consolidated profit and loss and the notes thereto provides opportunities for further analysis. Table 6.3 sets out turnover, each category of expense and each profit measure for the years 1990 to 1992. The meaning of figures in this 'raw' state is, however, rather difficult to grasp. Table 6.4 therefore expresses all the figures as percentages of turnover. A study of these two

Table 6.3. Turnover, Expenses and Profits, British Vita Group, 1990–92

Year ended 31 December	1990 £000	1991 £000	1992 £000
Turnover	635,948	694,276	788,528
Cost of sales	(476,990)	(527,600)	(602,698)
Gross profit	158,958	166,676	185,830
Distribution costs	(37,126)	(41,575)	(48,310)
Administrative expenses	(70,286)	(71,763)	(88,829)
Operating profit	51,546	53,338	48,691
Share of profit of associated undertakings	5,874	1,624	5,623
Profit on ordinary activities before interest	57,420	54,962	54,314
Interest receivable (payable)	(3,192)	(4,606)	842
Profit on ordinary activities before taxation	54,228	50,356	55,156
Tax on profit on ordinary activities	(21,081)	(20,322)	(21,216)
	33,147	30,034	33,940
Minority interests	(321)	(332)	(395)
Extraordinary items less taxation	2,040	—	—
Profit for the financial year	34,866	29,702	33,545

Source. British Vita PLC, Annual Report and Accounts, 1991 and 1992.

tables shows that although most figures have increased in absolute terms the percentage relationships between them and sales have changed only slightly; profit on ordinary activities and for the financial year 1992 are the same percentages of sales as in 1991: small percentage decreases in gross profit and operating profit to sales being offset, as already noted, by changes in interest receivable and payable.

With the help of the segmental analysis supplied in note 1 [p. 27] it is possible to analyse turnover both by class of business (cellular polymers, industrial polymers, fibres and fabrics, corporate and other) and by geographical origin (UK, continental Europe,

Table 6.4. Turnover, Expenses and Profits, British Vita Group, 1990–92
(turnover of each year = 100)

Year ended 31 December	1990 %	1991 %	1992 %
Turnover	100	100	100
Cost of sales	75	76	76
Gross profit	25	24	24
Distribution costs	6	6	6
Administration expenses	11	10	11
Operating profit	8	8	6
Share of profit of associated undertaking	1	0	1
Profit on ordinary activities before interest	9	8	7
Interest receivable (payable)	(0)	(1)	0
Profit on ordinary activities before taxation	9	7	7
Tax on profit on ordinary activities	(3)	(3)	(3)
	5	4	4
Minority interests	(0)	(0)	(0)
Extraordinary items less taxation	(0)	–	–
Profit for the financial year	5	4	4

Note. Percentages may not add to totals because of rounding.
Source. Based on Table 6.3.

international). This is done in Table 6.5. The charts on p. 4 of British Vita's report illustrate the 1992 figures for turnover by class of business and by geographical destination in pie chart form. This table clearly shows the increasing importance to the group of cellular polymers relative to industrial polymers and fibres and fabrics and of Continental Europe as a market relative to the UK.

Turning back to the profit and loss account as a whole, Table 6.6 shows the way in which each major item – turnover, operating profit, profit on ordinary activities before interest, profit on ordinary activities before taxation and profit for the financial year – increased

Table 6.5. Segmental Analysis of British Vita's Turnover 1990–92

Class of business	1990		1991		1992	
	£000	%	£000	%	£000	%
Cellular polymers	379,520	60	436,728	63	518,175	66
Industrial polymers	158,468	25	155,221	22	162,769	21
Fibres and fabrics	93,459	15	98,786	14	104,545	13
Corporate and other	4,501	1	3,541	1	3,039	0
	635,948	100	694,276	100	788,528	100
Geographical origin						
UK	242,843	38	242,896	35	253,941	32
Continental Europe	382,631	60	432,435	62	499,427	63
International	10,474	2	18,945	3	35,160	4
	635,948	100	694,276	100	788,528	100

Note. Percentages may not add to total because of rounding.
Source. British Vita PLC, Annual Report and Accounts, 1991 and 1992, note 1.

Table 6.6. Growth Rates, British Vita Group, 1991–92

	1991 %	1992 %
Turnover	9.2	13.6
Operating profit	3.5	(8.7)
Profit on ordinary activities before interest	(4.3)	(1.2)
Profit on ordinary activities before taxation	(7.1)	9.5
Profit for the financial year	(14.8)	12.9

Note. Percentages show percentage increase (decrease) over the previous year (1991 on 1990, 1992 on 1991).
Source. Based on Table 6.3.

or decreased in percentage terms in 1991 and 1992. This table confirms what has already been deduced: rising turnover in both years; operating profit rising in 1991 but falling in 1992; interest payments bringing down overall profit in 1991 but interest receipts pulling them up in 1992.

Table 6.7. Value Added Statement, British Vita, year ended 31 December 1992

		£000
Turnover[1]		788,528
Bought-in materials and services[2]		521,274
Value added (gross)		267,254
Investment income[3]		7,942
Share of profit of associated undertakings[1]		5,623
Value added available		280,819
Applied as follows:		
To employees[4]		194,172
To providers of capital:		
interest[5]	7,100	
dividends to British Vita shareholders[1]	15,296	
minority share[1]	395	
		22,791
To governments as taxation[6]		20,606
To retentions for replacement and expansion:		
depreciation[7]	25,001	
retained profit[1]	18,249	
		43,250
		280,819

1. As in the consolidated profit and loss account [p. 22]
2. Balancing figure equal to

		£000
Cost of sales[1]		602,698
Distribution costs[1]		48,310
Administrative expenses[1]		88,829
		739,837
less employment costs [p. 29]	194,172	
depreciation [p. 27]	25,001	
		219,173
		520,664
add government grants [p. 27]		610
		521,274

3. Interest receivable [p. 28]
4. Employment costs [p. 29]
5. Interest payable [p. 28]
6. Taxation in consolidated profit and loss account   21,216
   less   government grants received [p. 27]   (610)
7. As disclosed on [p. 27]   20,606

Constructing a Value Added Statement

Technically, a statement of value added is merely another way of displaying the figures for a year's operations but with the emphasis on gross value added (that is, turnover less bought-in materials and services) instead of profit. British Vita's for 1992 can be constructed as in Table 6.7. The notes explain where the figures come from.

Analysing the Value Added Statement

A number of useful ratios can be calculated from a value added statement. The ratio of value added to turnover, for example, provides a measure of vertical integration – that is, of the extent to which a group of companies produces its own raw materials and distributes its own products as distinct from buying these from outside. The higher the ratio, the greater the extent of vertical integration. British Vita's ratio (267,254,000 ÷ 788,528,000 × 100 = 34 per cent) is relatively low. Value added per £1 of employment costs is £1.38 (267,254,000 ÷ £194,172,000) and value added per employees is £2,698 (267,254,000 ÷ 9,904). (In making this calculation the employee of the associated undertakings are excluded [note 11, p. 19].) The more technically advanced an industry, the higher these figures are likely to be. We have already looked in Chapter 2 (p. 16) at the way, expressed in percentage terms, in which the value added is allocated among employees, providers of capital, taxation and retentions.

7. Liquidity and Cash Flows

> One may not doubt that, somehow, good
> Shall come of water and of mud;
> And, sure, the reverent eye must see
> A purpose in liquidity
>
> Rupert Brooke,
> 'Heaven'

Liquidity

It is very important that a company should be profitable; it is just as important that it should be liquid. In particular, companies which are profitable in the long term must make sure that they do not fail through lack of liquidity in the short term. An increase in profits must by definition lead to an increase in a company's net assets. There is no reason, however, why its liquid assets, such as cash in the bank, should automatically increase. A profitable and fast-expanding company may in fact find that it has tied up so much of its profits in fixed assets, stocks and debtors that it has difficulty in paying its debts as they fall due. To help prevent such a situation developing a company should prepare a cash budget – that is, a plan of future cash receipts and payments, based on specified assumptions about such things as sales growth, credit terms, issues of shares and expansion of plant. A simplified example demonstrating how a profitable company may run into liquidity problems is given below.

Oodnadatta Ltd is formed on 1 January to make boomerangs at a cost of £1.50 each and sell them for £2 each. All bills are paid immediately and debts are collected within thirty days. The stock of boomerangs manufactured and paid for in January, for example, will be sold in February and the cash proceeds collected in March. The company's provisional plans are to sell 400 boomerangs in

Table 7.1. Oodnadatta Ltd, Cash Budget and Budgeted Profit and Loss Statement

Budgeted Profit and Loss Statement

	Jan. £	Feb. £	Mar. £	Apr. £	May £	June £	July £	Aug. £	Sep. £	Oct. £	Nov. £	Dec. £	Total £
Sales	—	800	1,200	1,600	2,000	2,400	2,800	3,200	3,600	4,000	4,400	4,800	30,800
Cost of sales	—	600	900	1,200	1,500	1,800	2,100	2,400	2,700	3,000	3,300	3,600	23,100
Profit	—	200	300	400	500	600	700	800	900	1,000	1,100	1,200	7,700

Note. The sales figures are equal to the quantity sold multiplied by £2; the cost of sales figures to the quantity sold multiplied by £1.50; the profit figures to the quantity sold multiplied by £0.50. Note that the cost of sales figures give the cost of the goods *sold* during the month, *nor* the cost of the goods *manufactured* during the month.

Cash Budget

	Jan. £	Feb. £	Mar. £	Apr. £	May £	June £	July £	Aug. £	Sep. £	Oct. £	Nov. £	Dec. £
Balance at beginning of month	+ 600	—	— 900	-1,300	-1,600	-1,800	-1,900	-1,900	-1,800	-1,600	-1,300	- 900
Cash received from debtors	—	—	+ 800	+1,200	+1,600	+2,000	+2,400	+2,800	+3,200	+3,600	+4,000	+4,400
Cash payments to creditors	- 600	- 900	-1,200	-1,500	-1,800	-2,100	-2,400	-2,700	-3,000	-3,300	-3,600	-3,900
Balance at end of month	—	- 900	-1,300	-1,600	-1,800	-1,900	-1,900	-1,800	-1,600	-1,300	- 900	- 400

Note. Cash received from debtors is equal to the sales of the previous month; cash payments to creditors to the cost of sales of the next month.

February, 600 in March, 800 in April and so on. At 1 January the company has £600 in cash (raised by an issue of shares) – just sufficient to cover the manufacture of the first 400 boomerangs – but no other assets.

Table 7.2. Oodnadatta Ltd, Balance Sheets, 1 January and 31 December

Balance Sheets	1 January £	31 December £	Difference £
Cash	+ 600	– 400	– 1,000
Debtors	—	+ 4,800	+ 4,800
Stocks	—	+ 3,900	+ 3,900
	+ 600	+ 8,300	+ 7,700
Share capital	+ 600	+ 600	—
Retained profits	—	+ 7,700	+ 7,700
	+ 600	+ 8,300	+ 7,700

Note. The cash figure at 31 December is taken from the cash budget; the debtors represent the December sales, the cash for which will not be collected until January; the stocks represent the cost of goods manufactured and paid for in December for sale in January next.

Before actually starting production, the company draws up monthly budgets relating to profits and cash flows (Table 7.1). The figures show that although the planned profit for the year is £7,700, cash will fall by £1,000 from a positive £600 to a negative £400. There is thus £8,700 to be accounted for. We can see what will happen by comparing the balance sheet at 1 January with that which will result at 31 December (Table 7.2). The difference column shows the position quite clearly. All the profits, plus the original cash (£600), plus another £400 are tied up in debtors and stocks. It is interesting to note, however, that by the end of next January the company's liquidity crisis will be over:

	31 January
Balance at beginning of month	− 400
Cash received from debtors	+ 4,800
	+ 4,400
Cash payments to creditors	− 4,200
	£ + 200

The catch is, of course, that, as a result of its 'overtrading', the company is unlikely to reach next January in spite of its excellent profit-making potential, unless it can raise more cash by borrowing, by collecting its debts faster or by keeping down the size of its stock.

If sales continue to rise and costs also remain the same, the company will run into the opposite problem: excess liquidity. The purpose of drawing up cash budgets is to ensure that a company neither runs out of cash nor keeps cash idle when it could be profitably invested.

Current and Liquid Ratios

British Vita's cash flow statement was discussed in Chapter 2. In both 1991 and 1992 it shows a net cash inflow before financing. In 1991 cash and cash equivalents decreased by £5,169,000 during the year (mainly because of repayments of loans); in 1992 they increased by £57,891,000. Although much of the increase in 1992 was due to a new issue of shares, the statement suggests a general improvement in the group's liquidity. In the remainder of this chapter we look at several measures of liquidity.

Although cash budgets are an essential part of internal company financial management, they are unavailable to the external financial analyst, who must therefore use rather less precise measures of liquidity. What the analyst tries to do is to approximate the possible future cash flows as closely as possible. One crude measure of liquidity is the relationship between the current assets and current liabilities. This is known as the 'current ratio', and is defined as follows:

$$\text{current ratio} = \frac{\text{current assets}}{\text{current liabilities}}.$$

In calculating both current assets and current liabilities for the purpose of liquidity ratios, care must be taken to exclude any amounts falling due after more than one year. Current ratios can be calculated including or excluding short-term borrowings (including bank overdrafts and medium- and long-term loans which have reached their final year before repayment). The calculations for the British Vita group are explained in Table 7.3.

A more immediate measure of liquidity can be found by excluding stocks from the numerator. The resulting ratio is known as the liquid, quick or acid-test ratio:

$$\text{liquid ratio} = \frac{\text{current assets} - \text{stocks}}{\text{current liabilities}}.$$

The liquid ratio has the incidental advantage of being more easily compared among companies, since it does not depend, as does the current ratio to some extent, on the method chosen to value the stock-in-trade. Many analysts also exclude amounts owed by and owing to associated companies from, respectively, the numerator and denominator of the liquid ratio, and we shall follow this practice. The calculations for British Vita are explained in Table 7.4.

Table 7.5 analyses the composition of the current assets, looking at the relative proportions of stocks, debtors and cash (including short-term investments).

A number of conclusions can be drawn from Tables 7.3, 7.4 and 7.5. Firstly, the absolute size of the group's current assets has grown, especially in 1992. Secondly, that part which consists of cash and short-term investments has grown not only in absolute terms but also relatively to debtors and stocks. Thirdly, the general picture is one of increasing liquidity. This is in line with the group's strategy of making sure that it always has cash in hand to pay for acquisitions, but the group is perhaps running into problems of excess liquidity.

Table 7.3. Calculation of Current Ratios, British Vita Group, 1990–92

	Current assets as reported in balance sheet (a) £'000	Current assets excluding debtors falling due after more than one year (b) £'000	Current liabilities as reported in balance sheet (c) £'000	Current liabilities excluding short-term borrowings (d) £'000	Current ratio (e) = (b) ÷ (c)	Current ratio excluding short-term borrowings (f) = (b) ÷ (d)
1990	220,346	219,612	190,325	161,777	1.15	1.36
1991	232,514	232,023	211,213	159,080	1.10	1.46
1992	310,192	309,600	210,038	181,083	1.47	1.71

Source. British Vita PLC, Annual Report and Accounts, 1991 and 1992.

Table 7.4. Calculation of Liquid Ratios, British Vita Group, 1990–92

	Liquid assets (= col. b, Table 7.3, less stocks and amounts owed by associated undertakings) (g) £'000	Col. c, Table 7.3, less amounts owing to associated undertakings (h) £'000	Col. d, Table 7.3, less amounts owing to associated undertakings (i) £'000	Liquid ratio (j) = (g) ÷ (h)	Liquid ratio excluding short-term borrowings (k) = (g) ÷ (i)
1990	158,547	190,147	161,599	0.83	0.98
1991	170,385	211,045	158,912	0.81	1.07
1992	240,259	209,974	181,019	1.14	1.33

Source. As for Table 7.3.

Table 7.5. Composition of Current Assets, British Vita Group, 1990–92

	Total current assets %	Stocks %	Debtors %	Cash and short-term investments %
1990	100	27	56	17
1991	100	26	55	20
1992	100	22	46	33

Source. As for Table 7.3.

Defensive or No–Credit Interval

Both the current ratio and the liquid ratio are static rather than dynamic, that is, they treat liquidity as something to be measured at a point in time rather than over a period. A more dynamic approach would be to divide the liquid assets not by the current liabilities but by those operating expenses which require the use of liquid assets, namely, cost of sales, distribution costs and administrative expenses. Depreciation is not included as it is not a cash expense. What is sought is a crude measure of how long a company could survive without borrowing if no receipts were coming in from debtors. The calculations for British Vita are shown in Table 7.6.

The result of the calculations, measured in days by multiplying the ratio by 365, can be called the 'defensive (or no–credit) interval'.

Table 7.6. Calculation of Defensive Intervals, British Vita Group, 1990–92

	Liquid assets (= col. g, Table 7.4) (a) £000	Operating expenses requiring use of liquid assets (cost of sales, distribution costs, administrative expenses, excluding depreciation) (b) £000	Defensive interval (days) (c) = (a) ÷ (b) × 365
1990	158,547	565,288	102
1991	170,385	619,016	100
1992	240,259	714,836	123

Source. As for Table 7.3.

It would be preferable to use forecast rather than past cash expenses, but these, of course, are not available to the external analyst. The defensive intervals calculated in Table 7.6 confirm that the group became significantly more liquid in 1992.

Average Collection Period and Stock Turnover

Another important indicator of liquidity is the speed at which debts are collected. The average collection period for debtors can be calculated as follows, if one assumes that all sales are for credit:

$$\frac{\text{trade debtors} \times 365}{\text{sales}} \text{ days.}$$

Average debtors (defined as the mean of the opening and closing debtors figures) are also sometimes used. One problem with this ratio is that debtors include value added tax (VAT), whereas sales do not.

Another way of looking at the average collection period would be to think in terms of debtors turnover: $\dfrac{\text{sales}}{\text{average debtors}}$. The rela-tionship between stocks and cost of sales is usually looked at in this way: stock turnover $= \dfrac{\text{cost of sales}}{\text{stocks}}$. In assessing these ratios, it must

Table 7.7. Calculation of Average Collection Period and Stock Turnover, British Vita Group, 1990–92

	Sales (a) £000	Trade debtors (b) £000	Cost of sales (c) £000	Stocks (d) £000	Average collection period (b) ÷ (a) × 365 days	Stock turnover (c) ÷ (d)
1990	635,948	110,305	476,990	59,898	63	8.0
1991	694,276	114,522	527,600	59,491	60	8.9
1992	788,528	126,128	602,698	67,678	58	8.9

Source. As for Table 7.3.

Table 7.8. Calculation of Average Payment Period, British Vita Group, 1990–92

	Cost of sales (a)	Trade creditors (b)	Average payment period (b) ÷ (a) × 365 days
1990	476,990	90,217	69
1991	527,600	90,073	62
1992	602,698	101,863	62

Source. As for Table 7.3.

be remembered that they are weighted averages. There are important differences per class of business and per geographical area which only more detailed accounts would reveal.

Table 7.7 shows how British Vita's average collection period and stock turnover can be calculated. The sales (= turnover) and cost of sales figures are taken from the consolidated profit and loss accounts and the stocks figures from the consolidated balance sheet. Trade debtors are taken from the notes relating to debtors. The average collection period is seen to be falling.

The average collection period relates to credit taken. A similar calculation for credit given can be made as follows:

$$\frac{\text{trade creditors} \times 365}{\text{cost of sales}} \text{ days.}$$

Table 7.8 shows how the average payment period for British Vita is calculated. Trade creditors are taken from the note relating to creditors.

It will be noted that British Vita's average collection periods are shorter than its average payment periods and that the latter has also fallen in recent years. The increase in stock turnover (i.e., decrease in the number of days stock is held) is in line with the movements in the average payment period.

Predicting Insolvency

The extreme case of illiquidity is insolvency, which occurs when a company is unable to pay its debts as they fall due.

Can financial ratios be used to predict insolvency in advance? Researchers in both the USA and the UK have approached this problem by examining the ratios of companies just prior to their insolvency. It is possible by the use of statistical techniques to calculate what is known as a 'Z-score' for companies based on a number of relevant ratios appropriately weighted. Companies with scores within a certain range are more likely to become insolvent.

As is usual in ratio analysis, it is necessary to use more than one ratio and the result is a guide, not a certainty. A company with a bad score is not certain to become insolvent, but only more likely to.

Window-dressing

We end this chapter with an illustration of a problem which arises from the nature of ratios, and can give rise to a form of creative accounting. Suppose that a company has current assets of £800,000, current liabilities of £500,000 and liquid assets of £550,000. Its *net* current assets and *net* liquid assets will therefore be £300,000 and £50,000 respectively. If we keep these *net* amounts constant but vary the gross figures using current assets to pay off current liabilities, then the current and liquid ratios will vary as shown in Table 7.9.

Table 7.9. Illustration of Window-dressing

Current assets (a) £000	Current liabilities (b) £000	Liquid assets (c) £000	Current ratio (a) ÷ (b)	Liquid ratio (c) ÷ (b)
800	500	550	1.60	1.10
700	400	450	1.75	1.12
600	300	350	2.00	1.17
500	200	250	2.50	1.25
400	100	150	4.00	1.50
350	50	100	7.00	2.00
301	1	51	301.00	51.00

This is one example of window-dressing, which may be defined more generally as any transaction the purpose of which is to so arrange affairs that the financial statements of a company give a misleading or unrepresentative impression of its financial position. The example is exaggerated to make a point, but it is important to note that, within limits, companies may be able to arrange their current assets and liabilities so as to have the desired ratios at balance sheet time.

8. Sources of Funds and Capital Structure

Les affaires, c'est bien simple: c'est l'argent des autres.

Alexandre Dumas, fils, *La Question d'argent*

Sources of Funds

The funds available to a company are obtained either from its shareholders or by borrowing. The former includes not only issues of shares but also the retention of profits. The latter range from long-term debt to trade credit. The composition at any time of these sources, and more especially the long-term sources, is referred to as the 'capital structure' of a company. Table 8.1 gives some idea of the relative importance of various sources for large UK manufacturing companies in 1990.

Four points in particular stand out from Table 8.1:

1. The most important source of funds is the ordinary shareholders, especially through the medium of reserves (which consist mainly of retained profits), but also through the issue of new shares.
2. Preference shares and minority interests are of small importance.
3. Loans are important, although well behind reserves.
4. Provisions for liabilities and charges (which include deferred taxation and pensions) are quite important.

The sources of funds of the British Vita group are disclosed in the balance sheets, the cash flow statement and the relevant notes. The continuing great importance of shareholders' funds is very clear. At 31 December 1991 the group balance sheet [p. 24] discloses shareholders' funds of £172,269,000 and borrowings of £27,795,000. A year later shareholders' funds have increased by 63 per cent to £281,575,000. The main reasons for this increase were the issue of new ordinary share capital at a premium in the amount of £75,167,000 (as reported in the cash flow statement) and the retained profit for the year of £18,249,000 (as reported in the profit and loss account).

Table 8.1. Sources of Funds, Large UK Manufacturing Companies, 1990

	£m	%
Ordinary shares	20,575	10
Reserves	98,032	46
Ordinary shareholders' funds	118,607	55[1]
Preference shares	3,520	2
Minority interests	7,134	3
Provisions (including deferred taxation)	31,856	15
Debentures, bank loans and convertible loans	40,150	19
Other creditors and accruals falling due after more than one year	13,082	6
	214,349	100

1. Does not add to total because of rounding.
Source. Calculated from *Company Finance*, Twenty-third Issue, 1992, Table 8.

Capital Structure

Is there such a thing as an optimal capital structure for a particular company? This is a question which has aroused much debate. In principle there probably is such a structure, but it is not simple in practice for a company either to discover what it is or to achieve it.

The main problem is to choose the best mix of debt (loans, debentures) and equity (ordinary shares, reserves, retained profits). There is no easy way of doing this. It is possible to list the factors which ought to be considered, but assessing the weight to be given to each remains very largely a matter of judgement and experience. The factors are:

1. *Cost.* The current and future cost of each potential source of capital should be estimated and compared. It should be borne in mind that costs of each source are not necessarily independent of each other. An increase in debt now, for example, may push up the cost of equity later. Other things being equal, it is desirable to minimize the average overall cost of capital to the company.

2. *Risk*. It is unwise (and often disastrous) to place a company in a position where it may be unable, if profits fall even temporarily, to pay interest as it falls due or to meet redemptions. It is equally undesirable to be forced to cut or omit the ordinary dividend (see the section below on dividend policy).
3. *Control*. Except where there is no alternative, a company should not make any issue of shares which will have the effect of removing or diluting control by the existing shareholders.
4. *Acceptability*. A company can only borrow if others are willing to lend to it. Few listed companies can afford the luxury of a capital structure which is unacceptable to financial institutions. A company with readily mortgageable assets will find it easier to raise debt.
5. *Transferability*. Shares may be listed or unlisted. Many companies have made issues of shares to the public in order to obtain a stock exchange listing and to improve the transferability of their shares. Such a procedure may also have tax advantages.

Cost of capital and risk are discussed in more detail in the next two sections.

Cost of Capital

Although a company cannot always choose what appears to be the cheapest source of capital, because of the need to pay attention to risk, control, acceptability and transferability, it should always estimate the cost of each potential source and the effect on the overall average cost.

A rather oversimplified approach is to work out first of all the cost of each potential source of capital. This is most easily done in the case of debentures. Suppose that a company can issue £100,000 10 per cent debentures at par, repayable at par in twenty years' time. The before-tax cost is obviously 10 per cent; the after-tax cost, assuming immediate payment and a corporation tax rate of 33 per cent, is 6.7 per cent. If preference shares are issued instead, the before- and after-tax rates would be equal, since preference dividends, unlike debenture interest, are not deductible for tax purposes. This explains why, since the introduction of corporation tax in 1965, many companies have replaced their preference share capital by loan stock.

The arithmetic becomes rather more difficult if the loan stock is not issued at par. In December 1970, for example, Imperial Chemical Industries PLC made an issue of £40 million 10.75 per cent unsecured loan stock 1991/6 at £98 per cent, payable £20 per £100 stock on application, £40 on 1 March 1971 and £38 on 29 April 1971. That is, for every £98 received over the period December 1970 to April 1971 the company promised to pay interest of £10.75 each year and to repay the stock at par (£100) between 1991 and 1996. It can be calculated that the yield to the last redemption date (1996) was a fraction under 11 per cent.

The real cost of issuing debentures is reduced during a period of inflation by the fact that the cash paid out by the company will be of lower purchasing power than the cash it receives at the date of issue.

Reckoning the cost of an issue of ordinary shares is more difficult. An analogous calculation to the one above would suggest that the cost is equal to the gross dividend yield, worked out as follows:

$$\frac{\text{current dividend per ordinary share} \times 100}{\text{market price per share}} \times \frac{100}{80}.$$

The purpose of multiplying by 100/80 is to allow for the tax credit.

Dividend yields may be most easily found from the stock exchange pages of the *Financial Times* and other newspapers. The *Financial Times* Share Information Service gives quite a lot of information about shares every day. The following typical entry has been extracted from the *Financial Times* of 10 August 1993 (referring to the day before):

	Price	+ or −	1993 high	low	Market capitalization £m	Yield gross	P/E
British Vita	253	+2	268	215	£544.7	3.5	15.6

This tells us (for the date in question) that the current market price of British Vita's ordinary shares (par value 25 p) is 253 p, compared with a high for the year of 268 p, a low of 215 p and a price the day before of 251 p. (Par values may be assumed to be 25 p unless the *Financial Times* states otherwise.) The market capitalization is a measure of company size calculated by multiplying the market price by the number of shares.

British Vita's dividend yield (gross) is calculated by the *Financial Times* as follows:

$$\frac{\text{current dividend per ordinary share} \times 100}{\text{market price per share}} \times \frac{100}{80}.$$

That is to say, given the 1992 dividend of 7.15 p per share [p. 1]:

$$\frac{7.15 \times 100}{253} \times \frac{100}{80} = 3.5\%.$$

The dividend yield of any company can be compared with dividend yields in general and with those of other companies in the same equity group or sub-section, by looking at the table in the *Financial Times* headed 'FT – Actuaries Share Indices'. On 9 August 1990 the dividend yield for 'Chemicals' was 4.14 per cent.

These yields can be contrasted with the 7.63 per cent yield on irredeemable government stocks and a redemption yield of 8.53 per cent on twenty-five-year redeemable debentures and loans reported in the same issue of the *Financial Times*. Given the relative riskiness of fixed-interest and variable-dividend securities, this is at first sight surprising. Before August 1959, in fact, the average dividend yield was higher than the yield on government stocks. Since then a 'reverse yield gap', as it is called, has existed. The main reason for the reverse yield gap is the realization by investors that equities offer more protection against the effects of inflation. This has raised share prices relatively and lowered yields.

The dividend yield cannot, however, be regarded as an adequate measure of the cost of equity capital. It fails to take account of the facts that future dividends may be different from the current dividend and that the price of the shares may change. Neither of these considerations is relevant to long-term debt with its fixed interest payments and fixed redemption prices.

Two possible measures of the cost of equity capital are the *earnings yield* and the *dividend yield plus a growth rate*. The earnings yield is calculated as follows:

$$\frac{\text{earnings per ordinary share after tax} \times 100}{\text{market price per ordinary share}}.$$

It is more usual to express the same relationship in the form of a *price–earnings ratio* (P/E ratio), which is simply the reciprocal of the earnings yield multiplied by 100, that is:

$$\frac{\text{market price per ordinary share}}{\text{earnings per ordinary share after tax}}.$$

In other words, the P/E ratio expresses the multiple of the last reported earnings that the market is willing to pay for the ordinary shares. The higher the P/E ratio (the lower the earnings yield), the more the market thinks of the company and the cheaper the cost of equity capital to the company. From the extract from the *Financial Times* it can be seen that British Vita's price–earnings ratio on 9 August 1993 was 15.6. How this calculation was arrived at is explained below.

As already noted, earnings are calculated after the deduction of tax and preference dividends. The tax charge, however, depends to some extent on the dividends declared, since there are both constant and variable components in the charge.

The statement of standard accounting practice on earnings per share (SSAP 3), which unlike most SSAPs applies only to listed companies, distinguishes between the 'net basis' and the 'nil basis'. The former takes account of both constant and variable components and has the obvious advantage that all the relevant facts are considered. The latter takes account only of the constant components (that is, it in effect assumes a nil distribution of dividends). Its advantage is that it produces an EPS which is independent of the level of dividend distribution. For most companies the two bases will in practice give the same result. This is not likely to be the case, however, for companies relying heavily on overseas income. SSAP 3 concludes that companies should use the net basis in their annual reports but should also show the figures arrived at on a nil basis where the difference is material. The *Financial Times* calculates P/E ratios on a net basis.

The 1992 calculation for British Vita is as follows:

$$EPS = \frac{\text{profit for the financial year less preference dividends}}{\text{weighted average of ordinary shares in issue during year}}$$

$$= \frac{£33,543,000}{£206,376,573} = 16.3 \text{ p.}$$

The P/E ratio on 9 August 1993 was therefore:

$$\frac{\text{market price per share}}{EPS} = \frac{253}{16.3} = 15.6.$$

Companies also publish a 'fully diluted' EPS figure where this is materially different from the 'basic' EPS. Dilution can arise from the existence of shares that may rank for dividend in the future, from convertible preference shares and loan stock, and from options and warrants (see below). British Polythene PLC, for example, reported in 1992 a basic EPS of 28.87 p and a fully diluted EPS, after taking account of the assumed full conversion of cumulative convertible redeemable preference shares and the exercise of options over ordinary shares, of 25.82 p.

Earnings are defined in the accounting standard to include all items of profit and loss including those of both a capital and a revenue nature. The Accounting Standards Board recognizes that companies may wish to publish EPS figures based on other, less inclusive measures of earnings (e.g., excluding items not related to trading performance) and a number of companies do this. In particular, the Institute of Investment Management and Research (IIMR) favours an EPS calculation based on 'headline earnings'. The *Financial Times* states whether or not price–earnings ratios are based on headline earnings.

The relationship between EPS and dividend per share (DPS) is known as the dividend cover. In its Annual Report [p. 5], British Vita reports its dividend cover for 1992 as 2.2, calculated as

$$\frac{EPS}{DPS} = \frac{16.3}{7.15} = 2.2.$$

Since the market is interested in future dividends, it prefers to see current dividends reasonably well covered by current earnings. This is some sort of guarantee that the dividends will be at least maintained in future since, if profits fall, there will be past retained profits to draw upon.

An alternative approach to the cost of equity capital is to add a growth rate to the dividend yield. If one considers, for example, that British Vita's dividends are likely to grow in future at an average annual rate of 5 per cent, then the cost of its equity capital would be estimated to be 3.5 per cent plus 5 per cent, which equals 8.5 per cent.

An approach to the cost of a company's equity capital strongly favoured in the literature on financial theory is that it is equal to:

$$R_f + \beta[E(R_m) - R_f]$$

where R_f is the return on a riskless security (for example, a treasury bill), $E(R_m)$ is the expected return on all the securities in the market and β (beta) is a measure of risk.

The meaning and measurement of beta is discussed in the next section.

Risk: Betas and Gearing

Risk is of two kinds: market (or systematic) risk and specific (or non-market) risk. Market risk can be quantified as the beta of a company's ordinary shares. Beta measures the sensitivity of the share price to movements in the market. British Vita's beta was estimated by the London Business School Risk Measurement Service (RMS) (July–September 1993 issue) to be 1.17. A beta of 1.17 means that the share will on average move 1.17 per cent for each 1 per cent move by the market. A share with a beta of 1.0 would on average move in line with the market. Betas as reported in the RMS ranged from 1.78 to 0.07. The beta of the Burton Group of multiple stores, for example, was 1.62. Industry betas are also available: 0.90 for plastic and rubber fabrication and 0.97 for multiple stores if the component companies are equally weighted.

Specific risk refers to factors specific to a company and is measured as a percentage return per annum. The higher the percentage, the greater the specific risk. Property companies tend to have a high specific risk and investment trusts a low one. Specific risk figures ranged from 124 per cent down to 7 per cent, with an average of 38 per cent. British Vita's and Burton's figures were 17 per cent and 41 per cent respectively. The industry figures were 32 per cent and 37 per cent on an equally weighted basis.

The distinction between market risk and specific risk is important because it is possible to reduce the latter by diversification (for example, by holding shares in both plastics and rubber fabricators and in multiple stores), but market risk cannot be diversified away. Both British Vita and Burton's are affected by the state of the economies in which they operate.

Betas can be measured from either market data ('market betas') or from accounting data ('accounting betas'). Betas do, of course, change over time, although most are reasonably stationary.

The more traditional accounting measure of risk is gearing. Companies with the highest betas tend to be highly geared and to come from highly cyclical industries.

Gearing (or 'leverage', as the Americans call it) is the relationship between the funds provided to a company by its ordinary shareholders and the long-term sources of funds carrying a fixed interest charge or dividend (for example, unsecured loans, debentures and preference shares). The degree of gearing can be measured in terms of either capital or income. A company's capital structure is said to be highly geared when the fixed charges claim an above-average proportion of the company's resources of either capital or income.

There are several ways of defining and calculating a 'gearing ratio' and it is always important to know which definition is being used. Whichever way the calculations are made, some companies are likely to be more highly geared than others, especially those which have relatively stable profits, and those which have assets which can be specifically identified and are not expected to fall in value over time, therefore providing good security. One definition of the ratio is:

$$\frac{\text{interest-bearing liabilities} + \text{preference shares}}{\text{ordinary shareholders' funds}} \times 100\%.$$

British Vita's interest-bearing liabilities are most easily defined as its borrowings falling due after more than one year. This figure as at

31 December 1992 is given in note 16 [p. 36] as £29,291,000. The preference shares capital amounts to £57,000. The calculation is therefore

$$\frac{29,291,000 + 57,000}{281,575,000 - 57,000} \times 100$$

$$= 10.4\%.$$

A similar calculation for 1991 produces a gearing ratio of 16.2 per cent. The main reason for the decrease in gearing is the issue of ordinary shares in 1992.

A stricter measure of gearing would include borrowings (bank overdrafts as well as loans) falling due within one year [see note 15, p. 34]. The argument is that bank overdrafts may be renewed each year and should therefore be treated as long-term sources of funds. This definition produces a gearing ratio for 1992 of 20.7 per cent and for 1991 of 28.4 per cent.

British Vita itself calculates gearing by the net cash method, which takes account of cash holdings as well as liabilities. If the former are larger than the latter, as was the case for British Vita in 1992, the gearing ratio will be negative. More usually (as in 1991 and earlier years [see p. 5] cash holdings will be smaller than borrowings and the gearing ratio will be positive. All methods show that British Vita became less highly geared in 1992.

All the above definitions are based on book values. Market values could (some would say 'should') be used instead if they are available. Our original definition would then become:

$$\frac{\text{market value of fixed interest securities}}{\text{market value of ordinary share capital}}.$$

'Times interest earned' is a different way of looking at gearing based on the profit and loss account rather than the balance sheet. It is defined as:

$$\frac{\text{profit before interest and tax}}{\text{interest (gross of tax)}}.$$

The lower this ratio, the more highly geared a company is.

Using the data on p. 4 of the 1992 report and adjusting for interest received [note 4, p. 28], times interest earned can be calculated for British Vita as follows:

$$1991 \quad \frac{54,962}{10,737} = 5.1 \text{ times}$$

$$1992 \quad \frac{54,314}{7,100} = 7.6 \text{ times.}$$

This measure also shows British Vita becoming less highly geared in 1992.

The major disadvantage of the 'times interest earned' method is that it ignores the existence of reserves, that is, the retained profits of previous years, upon which the company could call if necessary (if they are in liquid form). The same drawback applies to the 'priority percentages' approach, in which the analyst calculates the percentage of earnings that is required to service each category of loan and share capital.

The effect of gearing on profits available to ordinary shareholders can be seen from the following example.

X PLC is a very highly geared company and Y PLC a relatively low geared one. Their long-term sources of funds at the beginning of the year are as follows:

	X	Y
Ordinary share capital (par value)	100,000	200,000
Retained profit	100,000	200,000
Ordinary shareholders' funds	200,000	400,000
10% debenture	300,000	100,000
	£500,000	£500,000
Gearing ratio (debentures as percentage of ordinary shareholders' funds)	150%	25%

If profit before interest and tax during the year is £80,000 for both companies, the distributable profit will be as follows, assuming a 33 per cent tax rate:

	X	Y
(a) Profit before interest and tax	80,000	80,000
(b) Debenture interest (gross)	30,000	10,000
	50,000	70,000
Tax at 33%	16,500	23,100
Distributable profit	33,500	46,900
Times interest earned (a ÷ b)	2.67	8.00

Distributable profit will be 33.5 per cent of the par value for Company X and 23.45 per cent for Company Y.

If, however, the profit before interest and tax is £160,000, the position will be as follows:

	X	Y
(a) Profit before interest and tax	160,000	160,000
(b) Debenture interest (gross)	30,000	10,000
	130,000	150,000
Tax at 33%	42,900	49,500
Distributable profit	87,100	100,500
Times interest earned (a ÷ b)	5.33	16.00

Distributable profit as a proportion of the par value becomes 87.1 per cent for Company X and 50.25 per cent for Company Y. Note that while profits before interest and tax have doubled, X's distributable profit as a percentage of par value has gone up 2.60 times and Y's 2.14 times (because Y is less highly geared than X). It is clear that gearing enables a company to trade on the equity, as the Americans say, and to increase the ordinary shareholders' return at a faster rate than the increase in profits. The higher the gearing, the greater the relative rate.

Unfortunately, the converse also applies. Suppose that the profit before interest and tax falls to £30,000. The position will then be as follows:

	X	Y
(a) Profit before interest and tax	30,000	30,000
(b) Debenture interest (gross)	30,000	10,000
	—	20,000
Tax at 33%	—	6,600
Distributable profit	—	13,400
Times interest earned (a ÷ b)	1.00	3.00

The distributable profit as a proportion of par value of Company X falls to zero and that of Company Y to 6.7 per cent. If profits fell even further, Company X would not be able to pay the debenture interest out of its current profits and would have to call upon past retained profits (reserves). Once these were exhausted, it would be in serious trouble. Company Y is in a much better position to meet such an emergency. It must also be remembered, of course, that a company which has tied up its assets too much in fixed assets and stocks may run into similar problems even though its profits have not fallen. Profits are not the same thing as ready cash.

The moral is that companies whose profits are low or likely to fluctuate violently should not be too highly geared. Investors in such companies are running risks and will in any case prefer ordinary shares to fixed-interest debentures. From a company point of view the attraction of a relatively cheap source of funds must be balanced against the risks involved.

Dividend Policy

How does a company determine the size of the dividend it pays each year, or, putting the same question round the other way, how does a company decide how much of its profits to retain each year?

Retained profits are the most convenient source of funds, and a company which pays very high dividends loses this source and may have to raise money in the capital market. Issues of debentures and other loans usually have a lower cost of capital than either new issues of shares or retained profits, but, as we have just seen, there are dangers in a too highly geared capital structure. New issues of

Table 8.2. British Vita PLC: Earnings and Dividend Record, 1988–92

	1988	1989	1990	1991	1992
Profit for the financial year					
(£000)	22,693	29,795	35,187	30,034	33,940
Index (1988 = 100)	100	131	155	132	150
Earnings per ordinary share[1]	13.0 p	16.6 p	19.4 p	16.3 p	16.3 p
Ordinary dividend (£000)	7,350	10,203	11,724	12,476	15,296
Index (1988 = 100)	100	139	160	170	208
Dividend per ordinary share[1]	4.19 p	5.69 p	6.50 p	6.84 p	7.15 p
Dividend cover	3.1	2.9	3.0	2.4	2.2
Index of retail prices					
(average for calendar year)	106.9	115.2	126.1	133.5	138.5

[1]. Adjusted for capitalization and rights issues.
Sources. British Vita PLC, Annual Report and Accounts; Table 4.2 above.

shares are more expensive than retained profits because of the issue costs involved.*

On the other hand, most expanding companies will have to go to the market sooner or later, and one of the points that potential investors will look at is the dividend record. A company whose dividend has declined or fluctuated violently is not likely to be favourably regarded. For this reason companies prefer to maintain their dividends even if earnings fall. Dividends have an information content; that is, they alter or confirm investors' beliefs about the future prospects of a company.

On the whole, then, cost of capital considerations push companies towards constant or steadily increasing dividend payouts. Inflation may have the same effect if the directors of a company feel that the distribution to shareholders ought to keep pace with the decline in the purchasing power of money. It may also have the opposite effect if the directors feel the need to retain a higher proportion of historical cost earnings in order to maintain operating capacity. Two factors which may limit the size of the dividend are government policy and taxation. A number of governments since the Second World War, although not recently, in their efforts to

---

* Retained profits are not a costless source of funds. They can be regarded as a notional distribution of profits which are immediately reinvested in the company.

contain rises in wages and prices, have placed statutory limitations on the size of company dividends. In spite of capital gains tax, the British tax system still favours capital increases rather than income increases. There are many shareholders who are more interested in capital gains than dividends. In general, shareholders are likely to be attracted to companies which have a dividend policy suited to their needs. This is known as the 'clientele effect'.

We are now in a position to look at British Vita's dividend policy. Table 8.2 gives information about the group's dividend policy for the last five years. It has been adapted from the information given on pp. 4–5 of the 1992 Report. It is interesting to compare the earnings record with the dividend record. Profit for the financial year and EPS rose from 1988 to 1990 and then fell back as a result of the recession, whereas both dividends and DPS rose steadily throughout the period (see also the graph on p. 5 of the 1992 Report). In line with the practices of many companies, British Vita's policy has been to keep dividends rising steadily in money terms despite fluctuations in profits. As a result of this policy, the dividend cover fell from 3.1 to 2.2 over the period. A comparison of DPS and the retail price index shows that for the period 1988 to 1992 the former increased by 71 per cent, the latter by 30 per cent; that is, dividends per share rose in real as well as money terms.

Rights Issues and Capitalization Issues

Most issues of shares are either rights issues or capitalization issues. A rights issue is one in which existing shareholders are given a chance to subscribe before anybody else. If they do not wish to do so, they can sell their rights on the market. Rights issues have long been the norm, and since 1980 it has been obligatory for share issues by public companies to be rights issues unless the shareholders pass a resolution to the contrary.

British Vita has made both rights and capitalization issues in recent years. In 1992 the company made a rights issue: 35,416,471 new ordinary shares of 25 p each were offered on the basis of one new ordinary share for every five ordinary shares held on 4 March

1992. The offer price, fixed as usual a little below the current market price, was 212 p per share.

The effect of the rights issue on British Vita's balance sheet (ignoring the issue costs) was as follows:

	£000
Increase in cash balances (35,416,471 × 212 p)	75,083
Represented by	
increase in share capital (at par) (35,416,471 × 25 p)	8,854
increase in share premium (35,416,471 × 187 p)	66,229
	75,083

The purpose of the issue was announced by the board of directors to be to provide financing for future acquisitions and investments.

A capitalization issue (also known as a 'scrip issue' or a 'bonus issue') is simply a means of turning reserves into share capital. To clear up the misunderstandings which can arise from this, it is helpful to use a simple example. Consider a company whose summarized balance sheet is as follows:

Assets	150,000	Ordinary share capital (40,000 shares of £1 each)	40,000
less liabilities	50,000	Reserves	60,000
	£100,000		£100,000

The company decides to make a capitalization issue of one new share for two old shares. The balance sheet will now look like this:

Assets	150,000	Ordinary share capital (60,000 shares of £1 each)	60,000
less liabilities	50,000	Reserves	40,000
	£100,000		£100,000

All that has happened is a book entry. In order to increase the ordinary share capital from £40,000 to £60,000, the accountant has decreased the reserves from £60,000 to £40,000. The shareholders have not received any cash, only more paper. Are they any better off? In principle, no; the market price *per share* might be expected to fall proportionately. It may not do so, partly because unrelated factors may be affecting share prices at the same time, partly because the issue may have drawn favourable attention to the future prospects of the company. Of course, if the company announces at the same time that the total amount to be paid out in dividends to shareholders will be increased, then the shareholders really are better off and the market price will tend to rise.

Capitalization issues have to be adjusted for when making comparisons of earnings per share (EPS). In this example, if the earnings were £12,000 the EPS before the capitalization issue would be 30 p; after the issue it would be 20 p.

British Vita used part of its share premium in 1990 to make a capitalization issue; 57,966,003 ordinary shares of 25 p par value were allotted to existing shareholders fully paid, decreasing the share premium account (an undistributable reserve) by approximately £14,492,000 and increasing share capital by the same amount.

Convertible Loan Stock, Options and Warrants

So far in this book we have drawn a rather rigid dividing line between debenture-holders, who are merely long-term creditors of a company, and shareholders, who are its owners. It will have been apparent, however, that preference share capital has some of the characteristics of long-term debt. Another hybrid security of importance is the convertible loan.

The 1992 annual report of City Site Estates PLC, for example, includes the following item among the long-term loan capital: '7% convertible unsecured loan stock 2005/06 − £6.021 million.' The attraction of such stock to investors is that it enables them to buy a fixed-interest stock which they can later change into ordinary shares if they so wish. Whether they will make the conversion or not depends, of course, on the relationship between the market price of the ordinary shares and the conversion price at the conversion date. The investors' hope is that they have found a cheaper way of buying the ordinary shares than direct purchase. The disadvantage is that the rate of interest offered on a convertible loan is less than that on a 'straight' loan.

Why should a company issue convertible stock? There are at least two possibilities:

1. The company wants to issue debt and adds the convertibility as an added attraction.
2. The company would prefer to issue equity but feels that the price of its ordinary shares is temporarily depressed. By setting the conversion price higher than the current price, the management can, if its expectations are fulfilled, effectively make a share issue at the desired price.

The possible disadvantages to the company are that either the market price fails to rise and it is saddled with unwanted debt, or that the market price rises so quickly that it finds itself in effect selling equity more cheaply than it need have done. As already noted, the existence of convertible loan stock dilutes the basic earnings per share.

An option is a contract giving a right to buy or sell securities within or at the end of a given time period at an agreed price. Convertible loan stock is thus one form of option, as are also warrants (certificates giving the holder the right to purchase a security at a predetermined price at a future date or dates). British Vita, like most listed companies, grants options in its shares to both its directors and its employees. Details are given in the Notes to the Accounts [pp. 30 and 38].

Leasing

Instead of borrowing money to buy fixed assets, a company may decide to lease them; that is, to enter into a long-term contract which allows it the use of the assets (but does not give it the ownership) in return for a periodic rental. Early termination of the lease is penalized. Sometimes the company already owns the assets and raises cash by selling them and then leasing them back. This is known as sale-and-leaseback.

The effect in either case is similar to an issue of long-term debt, and it should be regarded and analysed as such. It is standard accounting practice for finance leases (leases that transfer substantially all the risks and rewards of ownership to the lessee) to be capitalized. This means that both the leased asset and the long-term liability to pay the lease rentals are shown in the balance sheet. Leases that do not transfer substantially all the risks and rewards of ownership to the lessee are termed operating leases and are not capitalized. Hiring and leasing charges have to be disclosed in the notes. British Vita discloses a figure of £3,043,000 in 1992 [p. 27]. The accounting treatment of leases by the group is explained on [p. 26].

As in all financing decisions, the effect on the tax payable by the company is an important factor in deciding whether or not to use leasing. If equipment is bought out of borrowed money, the company will be entitled to the capital allowances described in Chapter 3, and the interest on the loan will be tax deductible. If the equipment is leased, the lessor will receive the benefit of the capital allowances, but the lessee's annual taxable income will be reduced by the amount of the lease rental. It is not possible to state in general terms whether the tax effect will be favourable or unfavourable to the prospective lessee. Each case has to be analysed separately.

Off Balance Sheet Financing

Off balance sheet financing is the funding of a company's operations in such a way that under legal requirements and accounting standards some or all of the finance is not disclosed in its balance sheet. One effect of this will be to make a company look less highly geared than it really is. Off balance sheet financing can be achieved in many ingenious ways. Two examples are: the issue through a subsidiary of redeemable preference shares with a dividend equal to current interest rates (the preference shares will be shown in the *consolidated* balance sheet as minority interest, not debt); and the sale of goods by a company to a bank with a commitment or option to repurchase them at a *higher* amount (this can be argued to be a disguised bank loan, especially if the goods do not change their physical location). Off balance sheet financing obviously has the potential to mislead users of financial statements.

9.   Summary and Reading Guide

The reader who has come this far has already learned a great deal about the annual reports of companies, about financial statements and about accounting and finance. The purpose of this chapter is to summarize what has been learned and to make suggestions about further reading.

Companies

Chapter 1 was mainly about companies, the most important form of business organization in modern Britain. Just under 99 per cent of all companies are private, but public companies are of greater economic significance. It is with public companies, and especially with those that are listed on the stock exchange, that investors are mainly concerned. Published annual reports are typically those of groups of companies, consisting of a parent company, subsidiaries, sub-subsidiaries and associated undertakings.

Companies operate within the legal framework of the Companies Act 1985 and relevant case law. There are many good textbooks on company law. The most readable, although not the shortest, is *Gower's Principles of Modern Company Law* (Sweet & Maxwell, 5th edn, 1992).

Financial Statements

Chapter 2 dealt with financial statements. The three most important statements are:

1. *The balance sheet*, which shows the assets, the liabilities and the shareholders' funds at a particular date.
2. *The profit and loss account* (or income statement), which shows for an accounting period the revenues, expenses, net profit (before and after taxation) and often also the distribution of the profit.
3. *The cash flow statement* which shows the cash flows of a company over the same accounting period.

Assets are classified into *fixed* and *current*, and liabilities classified according to whether they fall due within one year or more than one year. The excess of current assets over current liabilities is the working capital of a company. Tangible fixed assets are depreciated over their estimated economic lives, depreciation in its accounting sense normally referring to the allocation over time of the cost less estimated scrap value.

Long-term sources of funds of companies can be divided into *loans and other borrowings* (including debentures) on the one hand and *shareholders' funds* (share capital and reserves) on the other. There is an important distinction between preference shares, usually carrying a fixed dividend rate and having priority in a winding up, and ordinary shares. The par or face value of a share is not necessarily the same as its issue price (issues are often made at a premium) or its market price.

The profit and loss account is drawn up from the point of view of the shareholders and discloses items such as turnover, cost of sales, gross profit, operating profit, profit on ordinary activities before interest, profit on ordinary activities before and after taxation, profit for the financial year and retained profit for the financial year. The same underlying data can be used to prepare a statement of value added, which shows how wealth has been created by the operations of the group and how that wealth has been allocated.

The cash flow statement demonstrates among other things the difference between increases in profit and increases in cash balances. Cash flow is a rather imprecise term, often meaning simply net profit plus depreciation and other items not involving the movement of funds.

A good introductory book on accounting and financial statements is C. Nobes, *Introduction to Financial Accounting* (Routledge, 3rd edn, 1992). At a more advanced and detailed level, the latest editions of D. Chopping and L. Skerratt, *Implementing GAAP* (Accountancy Books) and M. Davies, R. Paterson and A. Wilson, *UK GAAP* (Macmillan, for Ernst & Young) are invaluable.

Taxation

Chapter 3 dealt briefly with taxation and audit. Companies pay corporation tax, not income tax. Taxable income is measured in a somewhat similar way to accounting profit, with the major exception of capital allowances (which replace depreciation). The corporation tax rate refers to a financial year which ends on 31 March, but companies are assessed on the basis of their own accounting periods.

Under the UK's imputation system, companies pay advance corporation tax when a dividend is paid and the shareholder receives a tax credit.

In general, taxable income has tended to be less than accounting profit. The total amount of taxation so 'deferred' is disclosed in the notes but only included in the balance sheet to the extent that it is regarded as a liability.

Books on taxation tend to be written either for accountants (lots of figures), for lawyers (lots of case law) or for economists (lots of diagrams). Two books rather more readable and stimulating than most are J. A. Kay and M. A. King, *The British Tax System* (Oxford University Press, 5th edn, 1990), and S. James and C. Nobes, *The Economics of Taxation* (Prentice Hall, 4th edn, 1992).

Audit

The main function of the auditors of a company is to report to the shareholders whether in their opinion the financial statements show a true and fair view. A good introductory book is T. A. Lee, *Corporate Auditing Theory* (Chapman & Hall, 1993). The text of auditing standards and guidelines are set out in the latest edition of *Auditing and Reporting* (Institute of Chartered Accountants in Eng-

land and Wales). For further information see the latest edition of
P. Chidgey and J. Mitchell, *Implementing GAAS* (Accountancy
Books). A discussion of how auditing can be improved can be
found in W. M. McInnes, ed., *Auditing into the Twenty-first Century*
(Institute of Chartered Accountants of Scotland, 1993).

Regulation, Formats, Accounting Standards and Inflation

Regulation, formats, accounting standards and inflation accounting
were discussed in Chapter 4.

In Britain, decisions about disclosure, presentation and valuation
are mainly in the hands of the government, through company law,
and the accountants, through accounting standards issued by the
Accounting Standards Board.

Financial statements are based mainly on historical costs modified
by prudence and by the revaluation of fixed assets.

As noted in Chapter 5, all extant accounting standards and
exposure drafts are reproduced in *Accounting Standards*, revised annually and published by the Institute of Chartered Accountants in
England and Wales. The best short book on inflation accounting is
G. Whittington, *Inflation Accounting: An Introduction to the Debate*
(Cambridge University Press, 1983). A number of classic articles are
brought together in R. H. Parker, G. C. Harcourt and G. Whittington, eds., *Readings in the Concept and Measurement of Income* (Philip
Allan, 2nd edn, 1986).

Tools of Analysis

Chapter 5 was concerned with defining and explaining the uses and
limitations of ratios, percentages and yields as tools for the analysis
of financial statements. George Foster, *Financial Statement Analysis*
(Prentice-Hall, 2nd edn, 1986) and B. Rees, *Financial Analysis*
(Prentice-Hall, 1990) are very thorough treatments of the subject.
There are relevant chapters in John Sizer, *An Insight into Management
Accounting* (Penguin, 3rd edn, 1989).

Profitability, Return on Investment and Value Added

Profitability, return on investment and value added were discussed in Chapter 6, in which the relationships between sales, profits and assets were considered.

Liquidity and Cash Flows

In Chapter 7 it was pointed out that a company must be liquid as well as profitable and that making profits is not the same as accumulating cash. It was shown that the best way to control liquidity from inside the company is by means of a cash budget. The external analyst uses the current ratio and the liquid ratio as rather cruder measures. Other indicators of liquidity are the defensive interval, the average collection period and stock turnover. The extreme case of illiquidity is insolvency; some success has been achieved in predicting this by means of financial ratios.

Sources of Funds and Capital Structure

Chapter 8 discussed sources of funds and capital structure. It was pointed out that shareholders are still the most important source of long-term funds, especially through the medium of retained profits, but that loans and other borrowings are also of importance.

The problem of capital structure is to obtain the best mix of debt and equity. Factors to be considered are cost, risk, control, acceptability and transferability. It was argued that either the earnings yield (reciprocal of the price–earnings ratio) or the dividend yield plus a growth rate are better measures of the cost of equity than the dividend yield itself. The imputation system of corporate taxation has greatly complicated the calculation of measures of earnings per share.

Risk can be approached through traditional measures of gearing or through the calculation of betas, which quantify the market risk of a share as distinguished from its specific risk.

In deciding on its dividend policy, a company looks at its effect on the cost of capital, on dividend yield and on dividend cover, and has to take account of government policy, inflation and taxation. Most companies try to pay a constant or moderately increased dividend (in money terms) each year, ironing out fluctuations in earnings.

Rights issues give existing shareholders the first chance to subscribe to new issues. They are distinguished from bonus issues, where the existing shareholders receive extra shares without further subscription.

After explanations of convertible loan stock, options, warrants and leasing, the chapter ended with a brief discussion of off balance sheet financing.

There are a number of good books on the topics discussed in Chapters 6, 7 and 8. Readers of the financial press should consult R. Vaitilingam, *The Financial Times Guide to Using the Financial Pages* (Financial Times/Pitman Publishing, 1993). Two well-established textbooks are J. M. Samuels and F. M. Wilkes, *Management of Company Finance* (Van Nostrand Reinhold, 4th edn, 1986), and R. A. Brealey and S. Myers, *Principles of Corporate Finance* (McGraw-Hill, 4th edn, 1991).

Personal Investment

This book has not dealt, except incidentally, with problems of personal investment. Its primary purpose has been to explain and interpret company annual reports and financial statements, not to advise the reader directly on how to invest his or her money on the stock market. It is not perhaps out of place, however, to conclude by recommending a book which does do this: J. Rutterford, *Introduction to Stock Exchange Investment* (Macmillan, 2nd edn, 1993).

Appendix A. Debits and Credits (Double Entry)

Welche Vorteile gewährt die doppelte Buchhaltung dem Kaufmanne!

Johann Wolfgang von Goethe,
Wilhelm Meisters Lehrjahre, I, x

Most people know that accountants are concerned with debits and credits. Since it is possible to learn quite a lot about accounting and finance without using these terms, it has not been thought necessary to explain their meaning within the body of this book. Very little extra effort is required, however, to understand the underlying principles of double entry, so a brief explanation is given in this appendix.

It will be remembered from Chapter 2 that

$$\text{assets} = \text{liabilities} + \text{shareholders' funds.}$$

An increase on the left-hand side of this equation is called a debit (abbreviated to Dr.), an increase on the right-hand side a credit (abbreviated to Cr.). Similarly, decreases on the left-hand side are credits, and decreases on the right-hand side are debits. Debit and credit are used here as technical terms and should not be confused with any other meanings of these words.

It will also be remembered that shareholders' funds can be increased by the retention of profits and that retained profits is equal to revenues less expenses, tax and dividends. Now, since increases in retained profits are credits, it follows that increases in revenues are also credits, whereas increases in expenses, taxes and dividends must be debits. Conversely, decreases in revenues are debits and decreases in expenses, taxes and dividends are credits.

We can sum up the rules as follows:

DEBITS ARE:		CREDITS ARE:	
Increases in:	assets	Increases in:	liabilities
	expenses		share capital
	taxes		revenues
	dividends		
Decreases in:	liabilities	Decreases in:	assets
	share capital		expenses
	revenues		taxes
			dividends

It seems curious at first sight that both increases in assets and in expenses are debits. In fact, assets and expenses are much more closely linked than is usually realized. If a company buys for cash a machine which is expected to last ten years, it is rightly regarded as having acquired the asset machine (increase in machines, therefore debit 'machines') in exchange for the asset cash (decrease in cash, therefore credit 'cash'). Suppose, however, that technological change is so rapid that these machines have an economic life of only one year or less. Then, if the accounting period is one year, the machine can be regarded as an expense of the period (therefore, debit 'machine expense', credit 'cash'). Thus, in one sense, an asset is merely an expense paid for in advance which needs to be spread over several accounting periods in the form of depreciation.

The system of debits and credits is referred to as double entry, since maintenance of the accounting equation requires that any increase or decrease in one item be balanced by a corresponding increase or decrease in another item or items. There are always two sides to any transaction. Suppose, for example, that a company decreases its cash by £100. The other side of the transaction might be:

1. An increase in another asset such as a machine (so, debit 'machine', credit 'cash').
2. A decrease in a liability, such as a trade creditor (so, debit 'creditor', credit 'cash').
3. An increase in a negative shareholders' funds item such as expenses, taxes or dividends (so, debit 'expenses', 'taxes' or 'dividends', credit 'cash').

Note that cash is always credited (since the asset cash has been decreased) and that a negative credit is the same as a debit (and a negative debit the same as a credit).

Appendix B. Glossary of Accounting and Financial Terms

This glossary serves two purposes:

1. To collect in alphabetical order various definitions, descriptions and explanations scattered throughout the text.
2. To provide certain *additional* information, especially concerning those matters which must by law be disclosed in the published financial statements of companies.

For more detail see R. H. Parker, *Macmillan Dictionary of Accounting* (Macmillan Press, 2nd edn, 1992).

Abbreviated accounts. Financial statements in which advantage has been taken of the exemptions available to SMALL COMPANIES and MEDIUM COMPANIES.

Accelerated depreciation. The writing off of depreciation (e.g., for tax purposes) at a faster rate than is justified by the rate of use of the asset concerned.

Accounting concepts. The assumptions which underlie periodic financial statements. Examples explained in this glossary are ACCRUALS, CONSISTENCY, GOING CONCERN, OBJECTIVITY, PRUDENCE and SUBSTANCE OVER FORM.

Accounting identity (or equation). Another name for the BALANCE SHEET IDENTITY.

Accounting period. The period between two balance sheets, usually a year from the point of view of shareholders and taxation authorities. Corporation tax is assessed on the basis of a company's accounting period.

Accounting policies. The accounting methods selected and consistently followed by a business enterprise. Companies publish a list of accounting policies in their annual reports.

Accounting reference period. A company's accounting period as notified to the REGISTRAR OF COMPANIES.

Accounting standards. See FINANCIAL REPORTING STANDARDS; STATEMENTS OF STANDARD ACCOUNTING PRACTICE.

Accounting Standards Board (ASB). The body prescribed in the UK by company law as a standard setting body. It issues FINANCIAL REPORTING STANDARDS and has endorsed the STATEMENTS OF STANDARD ACCOUNTING PRACTICE issued by its predecessor, the ACCOUNTING STANDARDS COMMITTEE.

Accounting Standards Committee (ASC). A committee established by the major professional accountancy bodies in the UK and Ireland which, from 1970 to 1990, prepared STATEMENTS OF STANDARD ACCOUNTING PRACTICE.

Accounts payable. Amounts owing to a company; usually called debtors in Britain.

Accounts receivable. Amounts owing to a company; usually called debtors in Britain.

Accruals. The accounting concept that revenues are recognized as they are earned or incurred, not as money is received (accruals basis of accounting as distinct from cash basis).

Accumulated depreciation. The cumulative amount of depreciation written off a fixed asset at a balance sheet date.

Acid test. Another name for the LIQUID RATIO.

Acquisition accounting. A system of accounting which assumes the acquisition of one company by another rather than their merger. Compare MERGER ACCOUNTING.

Advance Corporation Tax (ACT). Tax payable in advance when a company pays a dividend. ACT is normally recoverable. The difference between the total corporation tax liability and ACT is known as MAINSTREAM CORPORATION TAX.

Aktiengesellschaft (AG). The approximate German equivalent of the British PUBLIC COMPANY.

Allotment. The allocation of shares by the directors of a company following applications for them by intending shareholders.

Alternative accounting rules. The rules set out in the Companies

Act allowing the application to company financial statements of accounting valuations based on current cost.

Amortization. The writing off over a period of an asset (especially an INTANGIBLE FIXED ASSET) or a liability. Sometimes used synonymously with DEPRECIATION.

Annual general meeting (AGM). Meeting of the members (shareholders) of a company held annually at intervals of not more than fifteen months (but the first AGM may be held within eighteen months of formation). Usual business transacted: reception of directors' report and accounts; declaration of dividend; election of directors; appointment of auditors.

Annual report. Report made annually by the directors of a company to its shareholders. Its contents are largely determined by company law and accounting standards.

Annual return. Document which must be completed within forty-two days of the ANNUAL GENERAL MEETING and forwarded forthwith to the REGISTRAR OF COMPANIES. Main contents are:

(1) address of registered office;

(2) addresses where registers of members and debenture-holders are kept;

(3) summary of share capital and debentures, giving number of issued shares of each class, the consideration for them, details of shares not fully paid-up, etc;

(4) particulars of mortgages and charges;

(5) list of names and addresses of past and present shareholders giving number of shares held and particulars of transfers;

(6) names, addresses and occupations of directors and secretaries (and nationality of directors).

Copies of the financial statements, directors' report and auditors' report must be annexed to the return.

All the above can be inspected at the Companies Registries in Cardiff, Edinburgh or Belfast on payment of a fee.

Applicable accounting standards. ACCOUNTING STANDARDS issued by a prescribed standard setting body (currently the AC-COUNTING STANDARDS BOARD). Companies other than small and medium-sized companies must state whether their accounts have been prepared in accordance with such standards and give

particulars of any material departure therefrom and the reasons
therefor.

Application money. The amount per share or unit of stock
payable on application for a new issue of shares or debentures.

Articles of association. The internal regulations of a company.
They usually deal with: rights of various classes of shares; calls on
shares; transfer, transmission and forfeiture of shares; alteration of
share capital; general meetings (notice, proceedings); votes and
proxies; directors (powers, duties, disqualification, rotation, proceedings); dividends and reserves; accounts; capitalization of profits; audit; winding up; and similar matters.

Asset. Any resource tangible or intangible from which future
benefits are expected, and the benefits from which are controlled
by a company as a result of a past transaction or other event.
Examples include machinery, stock-in-trade, debtors, cash,
goodwill.

Associated undertaking. An undertaking other than a subsidiary
in which an investing group has a PARTICIPATING INTEREST and
exercises significant influence.

Audit committee. A committee appointed by a company as a
liaison between the board of directors and the AUDITORS. Audit
committees normally have a majority of NON-EXECUTIVE
DIRECTORS.

Audit expectations gap. The gap between what users expect from
AUDITORS and what they think they are currently receiving.

Auditing Practices Board. The body responsible for the issue of
AUDITING STANDARDS and auditing guidelines. Half of its members are practising auditors and half non-practitioners.

Auditing standards. Standards issued by the AUDITING PRACTICES
BOARD designed to give credibility to the independence, objectivity and technical skill of AUDITORS.

Auditors. Independent experts who report to the shareholders of a
company their opinion on the truth and fairness of published
financial statements. Their remuneration (including expenses)
must be disclosed. A person is eligible for appointment as the
auditor of a company only if he or she is a registered auditor
and is a member of a recognized supervisory body (e.g., one
of the three institutes of chartered accountants) and is eligible for

appointment under the rules of that body. The auditor must not be an officer or servant of the company or of a company in the group; a body corporate; or a partner or employee of an officer or servant of the company or a company in the group.

Authorized share capital. The maximum share capital which the directors of a company can issue at any given time. Disclosed in the balance sheet or the notes.

Average collection period. The average speed at which a company collects its debts:

$$\frac{\text{debtors} \times 365}{\text{credit sales}} \text{ days.}$$

Bad debt. An amount owing which is not expected to be received. It is written off either direct to profit and loss account or by way of a previously established provision for bad (or doubtful) debts.

Balance sheet. Statement of the assets, liabilities and shareholders' funds of a company at a particular date. The Companies Act prescribes a choice of two balance sheet formats and requires that every balance sheet shall give a true and fair view of the state of affairs of the company.

Balance sheet identity (or equation). The identity: assets *equals* liabilities *plus* shareholders' funds.

Bearer securities. Debentures or shares which are not registered and are transferable by simple delivery.

Beta. A measure of the market (or systematic) risk of a company's shares (i.e., the sensitivity of the share price to movements in the market).

Big six. The six largest public accountancy firms worldwide.

Bonds. Fixed interest securities such as government loans or (in the USA) company debentures.

Bonus shares. Shares issued to existing shareholders without further payment on their part. Also referred to as a scrip issue, a capitalization issue and (in the USA) a stock dividend.

Book value. The monetary amount of an asset as stated in the balance sheet and books of account.

Brands. A means of distinguishing a product (and sometimes its manufacturer or distributor) from its competitors. An INTANGIBLE FIXED ASSET.

Called-up share capital. The amount of the ISSUED SHARE CAPITAL which has been called up (i.e., the amounts shareholders have been asked to pay to date). Equal to the paid-up share capital unless there are calls in arrears or calls have been paid in advance.

Calls. Demands by a company for part or all of the balance owed on partly paid shares.

Capital allowances. In effect, the depreciation allowable for tax purposes. At times it has differed quite substantially from that charged in the published financial statements.

Capital employed. Usually refers to the total of shareholders' funds plus long-term debt, but may be used to refer to FIXED ASSETS plus NET CURRENT ASSETS.

Capital expenditure. Expenditure on FIXED ASSETS. The amount of contracts for capital expenditure not provided for and the amount of capital expenditure authorized by the directors but not contracted for must be disclosed.

Capital gains tax. A tax on individuals. Companies pay CORPORATION TAX on their capital gains, not capital gains tax.

Capitalization issue. *See* BONUS SHARES.

Capital redemption reserve. When shares are redeemed otherwise than out of a new issue of shares, a sum equal to their nominal value must be transferred to an account with this name. For most purposes the reserve is treated as if it were SHARE CAPITAL.

Capital structure. The composition of a company's sources of funds, especially long-term.

Cash budget. A plan of future cash receipts and payments based on specified assumptions concerning sales growth, credit terms, etc.

Cash flow. The flow of cash into and out of a company. Often used loosely to refer to net profit plus depreciation, which is the result of movements in WORKING CAPITAL rather than cash.

Cash flow statement. A statement showing a company's inflows and outflows of cash (including cash equivalents) during an accounting period. Can be prepared by the 'direct method' or the 'indirect method'. Cash flows are classified under the following headings: operating activities, returns on investing and servicing of finance, taxation, investing activities, financing.

Chairman's review (or statement). Statement made by the chairman of a company at its annual general meeting and often included in the annual report. There are no legal regulations relating to its contents, but it often contains interesting and useful information.

Close company. A company resident in the UK which is under the control of five or fewer participators, or of participators who are directors. Introduced by the Finance Act 1965.

Common stock. American term for ORDINARY SHARES.

Company. Rather imprecise term implying corporate activity. This book deals with companies registered under the Companies Act. The liability of such companies is limited (either by shares or by guarantee), except in the case of unlimited companies.

Comparability. An accounting concept which emphasizes ease of comparison of the financial statements of different companies at a point in time.

Conservatism. *See* PRUDENCE.

Consistency. An accounting concept which emphasizes consistency of ACCOUNTING POLICIES over time for a particular company rather than COMPARABILITY of the financial statements of different companies at any one point in time.

Consolidated balance sheet. Balance sheet of a group of companies as distinct from the parent company only.

Consolidated profit and loss account. Profit and loss account of a group of undertakings as distinct from the parent company only. A parent company need not publish its own profit and loss account as well if the consolidated profit and loss account discloses the requisite details (*see* PROFIT AND LOSS ACCOUNT) and also discloses what portion of the consolidated profit (or loss) has been dealt with in its accounts.

Consolidation of share capital. Combination of shares into larger units (e.g., combining two 50 p shares into one of £1).

Contingencies. Conditions which exist at the balance sheet date the outcome of which will be confirmed only on the occurrence or non-occurrence of one or more uncertain events. Contingent liabilities must be disclosed as a note to the balance sheet.

Convertible loan stock. Loan stock which may be converted at the option of the holder at a future date or dates into ordinary stock at given price ratios.

Copyright. A right to published material. An INTANGIBLE FIXED ASSET.

Corporate governance. The processes by which companies are governed, including the relationships between shareholders, directors (executive and non-executive), third parties (e.g., creditors) and auditors, and the regulation of the companies by the state.

Corporation tax. A tax on the profits of companies; not payable by individuals. The rate may vary. There is a lower rate for small profits.

Cost of capital. The cost to a company of obtaining funds for investment.

Cost of sales. The cost of goods sold during a period, calculated by adjusting cost of goods purchased or manufactured by the change in stocks. Also known as cost of goods sold.

Cost of sales adjustment (COSA). An adjustment made in CURRENT COST ACCOUNTING in order to base the cost of goods sold on the cost current at the time of consumption instead of the time of purchase.

Coupon rate of interest. The rate of interest on the par value of a debenture or bond. Not necessarily equal to the effective rate.

Creative accounting. The use of accounting to mislead rather than help the intended user. *See also* OFF BALANCE SHEET FINANCING; WINDOW-DRESSING.

Credit. *See* DOUBLE ENTRY.

Creditors. Amounts, representing either cash or a claim to services, owed to a company. A distinction is made between amounts falling due within one year (also known as CURRENT LIABILITIES) and amounts falling due after more than one year.

Cum. Latin for 'with'. A price so quoted includes any dividend (div.), bonus issue, rights or other distribution.

Cumulative preference shares. PREFERENCE SHARES entitled to be paid the arrears of their dividend before any dividend is paid on the ordinary shares. Any arrears must be disclosed in the notes.

Current asset. Those ASSETS that are not intended for continuing use in a company's business. Most current assets are either already cash or can reasonably be expected to become cash within one year from the date of the balance sheet. Examples include debtors, stock-in-trade. If the directors believe that any of the current assets will not realize their balance sheet values in the ordinary course of business, this fact must be disclosed. The alternative terms 'circulating assets' and 'floating assets' are obsolete.

Current cost accounting. A system of accounting in which assets are stated at the VALUE TO THE BUSINESS and current costs instead of historical costs are matched against revenues.

Current liabilities. LIABILITIES which are expected to have been paid within one year from the date of the balance sheet (e.g., trade creditors, proposed final dividend, current taxation).

Current purchasing power (CPP) accounting. A system of accounting which adjusts historical cost accounts for changes in the general price level.

Current ratio. Ratio of current assets to current liabilities. A measure of liquidity.

Current taxation. Tax payable within one year from the date of the balance sheet.

Debenture discount. Arises from issuing debentures at less than their par value. Disclosed in balance sheet to the extent that it is not written off.

Debentures. Loans, usually but not necessarily, secured on the assets of the company. Usually redeemable but may be irredeemable.

Debit. *See* DOUBLE ENTRY.

Debtors. Amounts owing to a company. They are classified for disclosure purposes into the following categories:

(1) trade debtors;
(2) amounts owed by group undertakings;
(3) amounts owed by associated undertakings;
(4) other debtors;
(5) called-up share capital not paid;
(6) prepayments and accrued income.

Any amounts which fall due after more than one year must be shown separately for each category.

Defensive interval. A measure of how many days' operating expenses can be paid out of liquid assets.

Deferred taxation. Taxation arising from timing differences between accounting profit and taxable income. The potential amount of deferred taxation payable is disclosed in the notes. Only deferred taxation which is reasonably likely to have to be paid within the foreseeable future is included in the balance sheet.

Depreciation. A measure of the wearing out, consumption or other reduction in useful life of a FIXED ASSET arising from use, effluxion of time or obsolescence through technology and market changes. Amount of depreciation charged must be disclosed. Usually measured by allocating either the HISTORICAL COST or REPLACEMENT COST less SCRAP VALUE of the asset on a STRAIGHT-LINE or REDUCING-BALANCE basis. The accumulated (provision for) depreciation is deducted from the cost in the balance sheet to give the net book value. Depreciation is neither a source nor a use of funds.

Depreciation adjustment. An adjustment made in CURRENT COST ACCOUNTING in order to base depreciation on current REPLACEMENT COST instead of HISTORICAL COST.

Deprival value. Synonym for VALUE TO THE BUSINESS.

Dilution. The decrease in control and/or earnings per share suffered by existing shareholders when a new issue of shares is wholly or partly subscribed to by new shareholders.

Directive. A statement adopted by the Council of Ministers on the proposal of the Commission of the European Community. Directives are implemented through national legislation.

Directors' emoluments. The disclosure requirements are very detailed and complex. In summary, these must be disclosed:

(1) aggregate amounts received by directors and past directors as emoluments, pensions and compensation in respect of services as directors and as executives;

(2) emoluments of chairman and of highest-paid director (if greater than chairman's);

(3) number of directors whose emoluments amounted to not more than £5,000, number of those whose emoluments amounted to between £5,001 and £10,000, and so on in bands of £5,000;

(4) number of directors who waived their emoluments and the aggregate amount waived.

(Note: Points 2 and 3 do not apply to anyone whose duties were discharged wholly or mainly outside the UK. Points 2, 3 and 4 do not apply if the aggregate of directors' earnings does not exceed £60,000.)

Directors' report. Annual report by the directors of a company to the shareholders which must disclose:

(1) a fair review of the development of the business of the company and its subsidiaries during the financial year and of their position at the end of it;

(2) proposed dividend;

(3) proposed transfers to reserves;

(4) names of directors;

(5) principal activities of the company and of its subsidiaries and any significant changes therein;

(6) significant changes in fixed assets of the company, or any of its subsidiaries;

(7) an indication of the difference between the book and market values of land and buildings of the company, or any of its subsidiaries, if significant;

(8) in relation to the company and its subsidiaries:

    (a) particulars of any important events which have occurred since the end of the financial year

    (b) an indication of likely future developments in the business

    (c) an indication of any activities in the field of research and development;

(9) interests in shares or debentures of group companies of each person who was a director of the company at the end of the financial year (this may be given, instead, in the notes to the accounts);

(10) totals of UK political and charitable contributions of the company (or, if any made by subsidiaries, of the group), unless together not more than £200; the amount and name of political party or person paid for each contribution for political purposes over £200;

(11) where the company's average number of employees over the financial year exceeds 250, the company's policy as to:

    (a) employment of disabled persons

(b) continued employment and training of persons who become disabled while in the company's employment

(c) otherwise for the training, career development and promotion of disabled people

(d) employee involvement in company affairs, policy and performance.

Listed companies are required by the stock exchange to give:

(12) an explanation of any material difference between the disclosed trading results and those given in any published forecast made by the company;

(13) the identity of independent non-executive directors, together with short biographical notes;

(14) extra information regarding directors' interests and service contracts;

(15) a statement of the substantial interests of any persons other than the directors in the share capital of the company;

(16) details of significant contracts in which directors or substantial corporate shareholders are interested;

(17) a statement of the reasons for any significant departures from standard accounting practice;

(18) a statement as to whether the company is a close company for taxation purposes.

Discounted cash flow. The present value of future cash receipts and payments (i.e., their value after taking into account the expected delay in receiving or paying them).

Distributable reserves. A company's accumulated realized profits so far as not previously distributed or capitalized, *less* its accumulated realized losses so far as not previously written off in a reduction or reorganization of capital. Public companies may pay a dividend only if the net assets are not less than the aggregate of the called-up share capital and undistributable reserves.

Dividend. That part of the profits of a company which is distributed to the shareholders. May be interim (paid during the financial year) or final (recommended by the directors for approval by the shareholders at the annual general meeting). The proposed final dividend is shown in the balance sheet as a current liability.

Dividend cover. The ratio between EARNINGS PER SHARE and the ordinary dividend per share.

Dividend policy. A company's policy on how to divide its profits between distributions to shareholders (dividends) and reinvestment (retained profits).

Dividend yield. The relationship between the ordinary dividend and the market price per ordinary share, usually multiplied by an appropriate fraction to allow for the TAX CREDIT.

Double entry. A system of recording transactions based on the BALANCE SHEET IDENTITY. Broadly, increases in assets and decreases in liabilities and capital items (including expenses) are *debits*, and increases in liabilities and capital items (including revenues) and decreases in assets are *credits*.

Doubtful debt. Amount owing that a company is doubtful of receiving. It is usual to establish a provision for doubtful debts which is subtracted from gross DEBTORS (after deduction of BAD DEBTS).

Earnings per share (EPS). Net profit attributable to the ordinary shareholders (after tax and preference dividends) divided by the weighted average number of ordinary shares. May be calculated on a NET, NIL or MAXIMUM BASIS. The 'basic' EPS may be supplemented by a 'fully diluted' EPS to allow for share options and convertible loan stock.

Earnings yield. The relationship between the earnings per ordinary share and the market price per ordinary share. The reciprocal of the PRICE–EARNINGS RATIO multiplied by 100.

Employee information. The following must be disclosed:
(1) total average number of employees for the year and a division of this total by categories determined by the directors;
(2) staff costs divided into wages and salaries, social security costs, and other pension costs.

Employee report. A corporate financial report to employees, published either separately or as a supplement to a house magazine. Usually also made available to shareholders and other interested parties. May include a VALUE ADDED STATEMENT.

Equity method. Method of accounting for investments in associated undertakings.

Equity share capital. Defined by the Companies Act as any issued share capital which has unlimited rights to participate in either the distribution of dividends or capital. Often more narrowly defined to mean ORDINARY SHARES only.

Ex. Latin for 'without'. A price so quoted excludes any dividend (div.), bonus issue, rights or other distribution.

Exceptional items. Items exceptional on account of size and/or incidence which derive from the ordinary activities of a business. Compare EXTRAORDINARY ITEMS.

Executive director. A director of a company who is involved in its day-to-day operations.

Exempt private company. No longer exists. Before the Companies Act 1967 it was essentially a family company with the privilege of not having to publish its financial statements. Compare SMALL COMPANIES.

Exposure draft. A draft FINANCIAL REPORTING STANDARD or STATEMENT OF STANDARD ACCOUNTING PRACTICE published for comment by interested parties.

Extraordinary items. Material items possessing a high degree of abnormality and which arise from events or transactions that fall outside the ordinary activities of the company and which are expected not to recur.

Financial instrument. A document representing a promise to pay (e.g., a promissory note), an order to pay (e.g., a cheque) or a certificate of indebtedness (e.g., a DEBENTURE).

Financial ratio. Relationship among items in financial statements.

Financial reporting exposure draft (FRED). An EXPOSURE DRAFT issued by the ACCOUNTING STANDARDS BOARD.

Financial reporting review panel. A review panel whose main task is to examine material departures by companies from company law and accounting standards. It has the power to apply to the court to enforce compliance with its findings.

Financial reporting standards (FRSs). Standards issued by the ACCOUNTING STANDARDS BOARD.

Financial statements. Statements showing the financial position (balance sheet), gains and losses for a period (profit and loss account), and cash flows for a period (cash flow statement) of a company. A few companies also publish a VALUED ADDED STATEMENT.

Financial year. Runs for corporation tax purposes from 1 April to the following 31 March. The most popular period for UK companies is 1 January to 31 December.

First year allowance. A CAPITAL ALLOWANCE granted in the first year of purchase of plant and machinery.

Fixed asset investments. Investments that are intended to be held for use on a continuing basis in the activities of a company.

Fixed assets. Those assets which are intended for use on a continuing basis in an undertaking's activities. Divided into INTANGIBLE FIXED ASSETS, TANGIBLE FIXED ASSETS and FIXED ASSET INVESTMENTS.

Fixed charge. A charge which is attached to some specific asset or assets.

Fixed overheads. Those overheads whose amount remains constant over the usual range of activity.

Flat yield. A YIELD which does not take account of the redemption value of a security.

Floating charge. A charge which is not attached to any specific asset but to all assets or to a class of assets.

Foreign currencies. The financial statements of foreign subsidiaries must be translated into sterling before they can be included in the consolidated statements. The method of translation, of which the most common is the 'closing rate method', must be disclosed.

Franked investment income. Dividends received by one British company from another, with the addition of the related tax credit. The dividend can be passed on to the shareholders of the recipient company without payment of advance corporation tax.

Gearing. The relationship between the funds provided to a company by its ordinary shareholders and the long-term sources of funds carrying a fixed-interest charge or dividend.

Gearing adjustment. An adjustment in current cost accounts intended to show the benefit to shareholders of the use of long-term debt, measured by the extent to which the net operating assets are financed by borrowing.

Gesellschaft mit beschränkter Haftung (GmbH). The approximate German equivalent of the British PRIVATE COMPANY.

Going concern. An accounting concept which assumes that an enterprise will continue in operational existence for the foreseeable future.

Goodwill. The difference between the value of a company as a whole and the algebraic sum of the values of the assets and liabilities taken separately. Recorded only when purchased. Purchased goodwill is either written off immediately to reserves or amortized through the profit and loss account over its economic life.

Goodwill on consolidation. The excess of the cost of shares in subsidiary and associated undertakings over the book value of their net tangible assets at the date of acquisition. Can only appear in a *consolidated* BALANCE SHEET.

Gross profit. The excess of sales over costs of sales.

Group accounts. Financial statements of a group of companies as distinct from those of the parent company only.

Guarantee, company limited by. A company the liability of whose members is limited to contributing a predetermined amount in the event of the company being wound up. Companies may be limited by guarantee or by shares, or be unlimited.

Harmonization. The process of narrowing differences in accounting practices, especially among countries.

Historical cost. The monetary amount for which an asset was originally purchased or produced. The traditional basis of valuation in published financial statements. Often modified in the UK by the revaluation of land and buildings. Favoured because it is more objective and more easily verifiable by an auditor.

Historical cost accounting rules. The rules set out in the Companies Act relating to the application to company financial statements of accounting valuations based on historical cost. Companies must follow either these rules or the ALTERNATIVE ACCOUNTING RULES.

Imputation system. System of corporate taxation under which all or part of the tax paid on distributed profits by the company is credited to the shareholders, thus mitigating double taxation.

Income statement. American term for PROFIT AND LOSS ACCOUNT.

Income tax. A tax on individuals; not payable by companies. Rates of income tax vary over time.

Industry ratio. An average ratio for an industry.

Inflation accounting. System of accounting which allows for changes in general and/or specific prices. *See also* CURRENT COST ACCOUNTING and CURRENT PURCHASING POWER ACCOUNTING.

Insolvency. An inability to pay debts as they fall due.

Institutional shareholders. Shareholders other than persons, industrial and commercial companies, the public sector and the overseas sector (i.e., financial institutions such as insurance companies and pension funds). Of increasing importance.

Intangible fixed assets. Non-monetary assets such as GOODWILL, PATENTS, TRADE MARKS, BRANDS and COPYRIGHTS which have no tangible form.

Interim dividend. *See* DIVIDEND.

Interim report. Report issued by a company to its shareholders during a financial year (e.g., quarterly, half-yearly).

Inventories. American term for stock-in-trade.

Investments. Shares, loans, bonds and debentures held either as fixed tangible assets or current assets. Listed investments must be distinguished from unlisted.

Investment trust. Not really a trust but a company whose object is investment in the securities of other companies. Compare UNIT TRUST.

Irredeemable debenture. A DEBENTURE which will never have to be repaid.

Issued share capital. The amount of the AUTHORIZED SHARE CAPITAL which has been issued; the remainder is the unissued share capital. The amount of the issued capital must be disclosed in the notes. Not necessarily equal to called-up or paid-up share capital.

Issue expenses. Expenses of making an issue of shares or debentures. Disclosed in balance sheet to the extent that they are not written off.

Issue price. The price at which a share or debenture is issued; not necessarily equal to the PAR VALUE.

Leasing. Entering into a long-term contract which allows the use of an asset in return for a periodic rental, but does not give ownership. Its effect is similar to financing the purchase of the asset by loan capital.

Leverage. The American term for GEARING.

Liabilities. Obligations arising from past transactions or other events and involving a company in a probable future transfer of cash, goods or services. They are classified for disclosure purposes into the following categories:

(1) debenture loans;
(2) bank loans and overdrafts;
(3) payments received on account;
(4) trade creditors;
(5) bills of exchange payable;
(6) amounts owed to group undertakings;
(7) amounts owed to associated undertakings;
(8) other creditors including taxation and social security;
(9) accruals and deferred income.

For each item which is payable wholly or partly after five years from the balance sheet date, there must be stated:

(1) the aggregate amount payable otherwise than by instalments;
(2) the aggregate amount payable by instalments, and the aggregate amount of instalments which fall due after five years;
(3) the terms of payment and rates of interest payable.

There must also be stated for each heading the aggregate amount of debts for which any security has been given and an indication of the nature of the security.

Listed companies are required by the stock exchange to show in addition, subdivided between bank loans and overdrafts and other borrowings, the aggregate amounts repayable:

(1) in one year or less, or on demand;
(2) between one and two years;
(3) between two and five years;
(4) in five years or more.

All companies must distinguish between current and non-current liabilities.

Limited liability company. A company the liability of whose members is limited by shares or by guarantee. If by shares, liability is limited to the amount taken up or agreed to be taken up; if by guarantee, to the amount undertaken to be contributed in the event of winding-up.

Liquid assets. Current assets *less* stock-in-trade.

Liquid ratio. The relationship between liquid assets and current liabilities. Also known as quick ratio, or the acid test.

Listed company. A public company listed (quoted) on a recognized stock exchange.

Listed investments. Investments which are listed on a recognized stock exchange or on any reputable stock exchange outside Great Britain. Must be shown separately in the balance sheet.

Loan capital. Funds acquired by non-short-term borrowing from sources other than the shareholders of the company.

Long-term debt. Long-term sources of funds other than equity (share capital and reserves).

Mainstream corporation tax. The difference between a company's total liability to CORPORATION TAX and advance corporation tax paid and recoverable.

Market capitalization. The total value on a stock exchange of a listed company's shares.

Market price. The price at which a company's securities can be bought or sold on a stock exchange. Not necessarily equal to the PAR VALUE or the ISSUE PRICE.

Materiality. An accounting concept that requires disclosure only of data that are significant enough to be relevant to the needs of a potential user.

Maximum basis. Method of calculating EARNINGS PER SHARE based on the assumption that a company distributes all its profits and is liable to pay advance corporation tax on them.

Medium companies. Companies with the privilege of filing abbreviated profit and loss accounts and notes with the REGISTRAR OF COMPANIES. 'Medium' is measured in terms of total assets, turnover and average number of employees.

Medium groups. *See* SMALL AND MEDIUM GROUPS.

Memorandum of association. A document which states:

(1) the name of the company;

(2) that the company is a public company (if such is the case);

(3) the situation of the registered office;

(4) the objects of the company;

(5) that the liability of the members is limited (unless the company is an unlimited one);

(6) the authorized share capital and how it is divided (or, in the case of a company limited by guarantee, the maximum amount to be contributed by members on winding-up);

(7) details of the subscribers (the persons 'desirous of being formed into a company').

Merger accounting. A system of accounting which assumes the commercial substance of a merger of two or more companies rather than the acquisition of one by another. Compare AQUISITION ACCOUNTING.

Minority interest. That part of a subsidiary company's shareholders' funds that is not held by the parent company. Usually shown as a separate item on the capital and liabilities side of a consolidated balance sheet.

Monetary assets. Assets (e.g., cash, debtors) which have a fixed monetary exchange value which is not affected by a change in the price level.

Monetary working capital adjustment (MWCA). An adjustment made in current cost accounting in order to take account of the effect of increased prices on monetary working capital (bank balances + debtors − creditors).

Net basis. Method of calculating EARNINGS PER SHARE which takes account of both constant and variable components in the tax charge.

Net current assets. Another name for WORKING CAPITAL.

Net profit. The excess of revenues over expenses. Calculated before or after extraordinary items and before or after tax depending upon the context.

Net profit ratio. Ratio of net profit to sales.

Net realizable value. The amount for which an asset can be sold, net of the expenses of completion and of sale.

Net tangible assets. Assets other than INTANGIBLE ASSETS *less* LIABILITIES.

Net working capital. Another name for WORKING CAPITAL.

Nil basis. Method of calculating EARNINGS PER SHARE which assumes a nil distribution of dividends.

No credit interval. Another term for DEFENSIVE INTERVAL.

Nominal share capital. *See* AUTHORIZED SHARE CAPITAL.

Nominee shareholder. A shareholder who holds shares on behalf of another person or company who is the beneficial shareholder.

Non-executive directors. Directors who take no part in a company's day-to-day operations.

Non-monetary assets. Assets other than MONETARY ASSETS (i.e., mainly fixed assets and stock-in-trade).

Non-statutory accounts. Financial statements prepared for a purpose other than as part of a company's STATUTORY ACCOUNTS.

Non-voting shares. Shares with no voting rights. Non-voting ordinary shares are usually cheaper to buy than those which carry votes. Often called 'A' shares.

No par value shares. Shares with no nominal or par value. They are illegal in Britain.

Note of historical cost profits and losses. A calculation of what a company's profit on ordinary activities before taxation and retained profit would be if based entirely on historical cost accounting without, e.g., any revaluation of fixed assets.

Notes to the accounts. Notes attached to and explanatory of items in the financial statements. May be very detailed.

Objectivity. Accounting concept which stresses the need to establish rules for recording financial transactions and events which so far as possible do not depend upon the personal judgement of the recorder.

Off balance sheet financing. Financing assets by 'borrowing' in such a fashion that the debt does not appear as a balance sheet item.

Operating and financial review. An analysis and explanation in an ANNUAL REPORT of the main features of a company's performance and financial position.

Operating profit. The excess of operating revenues over operating expenses, usually on an historical cost basis.

Ordinary shares. Shares entitled to share in the profits after payment of loan interest and preference dividends. Often referred to as the equity capital.

Overheads. Expenses other than the direct costs of material and labour.

Overtrading. A situation in which a company expands its sales and may appear to be highly profitable but does not have the resources available to finance the expansion and is therefore in danger of running out of cash.

Paid-up share capital. The amount of the CALLED-UP SHARE CAPITAL which has been paid up by the shareholders.

Parent undertaking. An undertaking that has one or more SUBSIDIARY UNDERTAKINGS. A parent undertaking of a group (other than a small or a medium group) must, if it is a company, prepare a CONSOLIDATED BALANCE SHEET and a CONSOLIDATED PROFIT AND LOSS ACCOUNT in addition to its own financial statements.

Participating interest. An interest in the shares of an undertaking which is held on a long-term basis for the purpose of securing a contribution to the investor by the exercise of control or influence arising from or related to that interest.

Par value. The face or nominal value of a share or debenture. Not necessarily equal to the ISSUE PRICE or the current MARKET PRICE. Dividend and interest percentages refer to the par value, YIELDS to the current market price.

Patents. Grants by the Crown to the authors of new inventions giving them the sole and exclusive right to use, exercise and sell their inventions and to secure the profits arising therefrom for a limited period. An INTANGIBLE FIXED ASSET.

Post balance sheet events. Events occurring after the date of the balance sheet. They are either 'adjusting events' (those providing additional evidence of conditions existing at the balance sheet date) or 'non-adjusting events'.

Pre-acquisition profits. The accumulated profits of a subsidiary up to the date of its acquisition (takeover) by the parent.

Preference shares. Shares which usually are entitled to a fixed rate of dividend before a dividend is paid on the ordinary shares and to priority of repayment if the company is wound up.

Participating preference shares are also entitled to a further dividend if profits are available. If a preference dividend is not paid, the arrears must be disclosed as a note to the balance sheet. Arrears can only arise if the shares are *cumulative* as distinct from *non-cumulative*.

Preliminary announcement. An announcement, obligatory for listed companies, of the annual results of a company made by the directors before the full, audited accounts are published.

Preliminary expenses. Expenses of forming a company.

Price–earnings ratio. The multiple of the last reported EARNINGS PER SHARE that the market is willing to pay per ordinary share. The reciprocal of the EARNINGS YIELD multiplied by 100.

Prior charges. Claims on a company's assets and profits that rank ahead of ordinary share capital.

Priority percentages. Method of calculating GEARING by computing the percentage of earnings that is required to service each category of loan and share capital.

Prior year adjustments. Material adjustments applicable to prior years arising from changes in accounting policies or from the correction of fundamental errors.

Private company. A company which is not a PUBLIC COMPANY. Not permitted to issue shares or debentures to the public.

Profit. A general term for the excess of revenues over expenses. *See* GROSS PROFIT and NET PROFIT.

Profit and loss account. Statement of the revenue, expenses and profit of a company for a particular period. The Companies Act prescribes a choice of four profit and loss account formats and requires that every profit and loss account shall give a true and fair view of the profit or loss for the financial year. A published profit and loss account includes appropriations of profit and is therefore a combination of a profit and loss account proper and a PROFIT AND LOSS APPROPRIATION ACCOUNT.

Profit and loss appropriation account. Continuation of PROFIT AND LOSS ACCOUNT proper giving details of profit appropriations (i.e., distribution as dividends and retention as reserves).

Prospectus. Any notice, circular, advertisement or other invitation offering shares or debentures to the public.

Provision. Either a PROVISION FOR LIABILITIES AND CHARGES or a valuation adjustment, i.e., an amount written off fixed assets (by way of depreciation or amortization) or current assets (e.g., a provision for doubtful debts). In both cases a charge is made to PROFIT AND LOSS ACCOUNT, but provisions for liabilities and charges are shown in the balance sheet as part of the liabilities, whereas valuation adjustments are deducted from the asset concerned.

Provision for liabilities and charges. Amount retained as reasonably necessary for the purpose of providing for any liability or loss which is either likely to be incurred, or certain to be incurred, but uncertain as to the amount or as to the date on which it will arise. Examples include pensions and deferred taxation.

Proxy. A person appointed to attend and vote at a company meeting on behalf of a shareholder, or the form, signed by the shareholder, which grants that authority.

Prudence. Accounting concept under which revenue and profits are not anticipated but are recognized by inclusion in the PROFIT AND LOSS ACCOUNT only when realized in cash or other assets, the ultimate realization of which can be assessed with reasonable certainty. Provision is made for all known liabilities, whether the amount of these is known with certainty or is a best estimate in the light of the information available.

Public company. A company whose MEMORANDUM OF ASSOCIATION states that it is a public company whose name ends with the words 'public limited company' (plc; ccc for Welsh companies) and which has a minimum authorized and allotted share capital at least one quarter paid up, of £50,000. Unlike a PRIVATE COMPANY, a public company is permitted to issue shares or debentures to the public.

Quasi subsidiaries. Companies which are legally not SUBSIDIARY UNDERTAKINGS of another company but are in fact controlled directly or indirectly by that company.

Quick assets. Current assets *less* stock-in-trade.

Quick ratio. *See* LIQUID RATIO.

Recognized supervisory body. An accountancy body recognized for the purpose of overseeing and maintaining the conduct and technical standards of company AUDITORS.

Reconciliation of movements in shareholders' funds. A statement of how the total of SHAREHOLDERS' FUNDS has changed during a financial year, e.g., by the retention of profits and the issue of share capital.

Recoverable amount. The greater of the NET REALIZABLE VALUE of an asset and the amount recoverable from its further use.

Redeemable shares. Shares which must or may be redeemed at the option of the company or (very rarely) the shareholder. The balance sheet must disclose the earliest and latest dates on which the company has power to redeem, whether at the option of the company or in any event, and also the amount of any premium on redemption.

Redemption yield. A YIELD which takes into account not only the annual interest receivable but also the redemption value of a security.

Reducing balance depreciation. Method of depreciation in which the periodic amount written off decreases over the life of the asset. A fixed percentage is applied to a declining written-down value.

Registered auditor. A person or firm whose name is inscribed on a statutory register as qualified for appointment as a company AUDITOR.

Registered office. The official address of a company. The MEMORANDUM OF ASSOCIATION must state whether it is in England, Wales or Scotland.

Registrar of Companies. Government officer with whom annual reports (including financial statements) and other documents must be filed; in Cardiff for companies registered in England and Wales, in Edinburgh for companies registered in Scotland.

Replacement cost. The cost of replacing an asset.

Research and development expenditure. Includes expenditure on pure research, applied research and development. Only the last is in some circumstances treated as an asset.

Reserve. Reserves arise either from the retention of profits or from events such as the issue of shares at a premium or the revaluation of assets. Must not include PROVISIONS unless the directors consider the latter are excessive. Not a charge against profits and not usually represented by cash on the other side of the balance sheet. Movements in reserves during the financial year must be disclosed.

Reserve fund. A RESERVE which is represented by specially earmarked cash or investments on the other side of the balance sheet.

Retained profits. Profits not distributed to shareholders but reinvested in the company. Their cost is less than a new issue of shares because of the issue costs of the latter.

Return on investment. Ratio of profit (usually before interest and tax) to NET TANGIBLE ASSETS. A measure of profitability.

Revaluation. The writing-up of an asset to its current market value.

Revaluation reserve. The amount of gain or loss arising from the revaluation of any asset. An undistributable reserve unless the profit or loss has been realized.

Revenue expenditure. Expenditure that is written off completely in the PROFIT AND LOSS ACCOUNT in the accounting period in which it is made.

Reverse yield gap. A description of the fact that since August 1959 the average yield on government bonds has been greater than the average dividend yield on the ordinary shares of companies, despite the greater (monetary) security of the former.

Rights issue. An issue of shares in which the existing shareholders have a right to subscribe for the new shares at a stated price. The right can be sold if the shareholder does not wish to subscribe.

Risk. *See* SYSTEMATIC RISK and SPECIFIC RISK.

Sale and leaseback. Raising cash by selling an asset and then leasing it back in a long-term contract. *See also* LEASING.

Scrap value. The amount at which a FIXED ASSET is expected to be sold at the end of its estimated economic life.

Scrip issue. *See* BONUS SHARES.

Securities and Exchange Commission (SEC). American federal body concerned with the operations of corporations (i.e., companies) and issues of and dealings in their securities. It has the right, which it has largely allowed the Financial Accounting Standards Board to exercise, to establish accounting principles.

Security. Two meanings: (1) A generic name for stock, shares, debentures, etc. (2) The backing for a loan.

Segment reporting. Reporting the results of a diversified group of companies by major classes of business and geographical area. The Companies Act requires disclosure in the notes of turnover and profit or loss before taxation attributable to each class of business that, in the opinion of the directors, differs substantially from any other class. Turnover must also be disclosed by geographical markets where, in the opinion of the directors, these differ substantially from each other. ACCOUNTING STANDARDS extend these requirements for public companies, banking and insurance companies, and the larger private companies, requiring for both business and geographical segments the disclosure of turnover, profit or loss (before tax, minority interests and extraordinary items), and net assets.

Share capital. Unless limited by guarantee, a company registered under the Companies Act must have a share capital divided into shares of a fixed amount. The ownership of a share gives the shareholder a proportionate ownership of the company. The share capital is stated in the balance sheet at its par (nominal) value.

Shareholder. Member of a company whose part ownership of (share in) the company is evidenced by a share certificate.

Shareholders' funds. The proprietorship section of a company balance sheet. Includes the share capital and the reserves. Also known as shareholders' equity.

Share option. The right to buy or sell shares within a stated period.

Share premium. Results from issuing shares at a price higher than their par value. Must be disclosed in the balance sheet as a RESERVE. Cannot be used to pay dividends but can be used to make an issue of BONUS SHARES.

Simplified financial statements. Financial statements prepared so that those unskilled in accounting may more readily understand them. *See also* SUMMARY FINANCIAL STATEMENTS.

Small and medium groups. Groups of companies which are exempt from preparing and filing GROUP ACCOUNTS with the REGISTRAR OF COMPANIES. 'Small' and 'medium' are measured in terms of total assets, turnover and average number of employees.

Small companies. Companies with the privilege of preparing an abbreviated balance sheet and notes and not preparing a profit and loss account and directors' report. 'Small' is measured in terms of total assets, turnover and average number of employees.

Small companies rate. A reduced rate of corporation tax paid by companies with small taxable incomes. This tax relief is not related to small companies as defined in the Companies Act.

Société anonyme (SA). The approximate French equivalent of a British PUBLIC COMPANY.

Société à responsabilité limitée (SARL). The approximate French equivalent of a British PRIVATE COMPANY.

Solvency. The ability of a debtor to pay debts as they fall due.

Source and application of funds, statement of. A statement showing the sources of funds (e.g., new issue of shares or debentures, retained profits) and the uses of funds (e.g., purchase of new fixed assets, increase in working capital) of a company over a period.

Specific prices. The prices, observable in a market, of specific goods and services. The government provides specific price indices periodically in its publication *Price Index Numbers for Current Cost Accounting*.

Specific risk. Risk arising from factors specific to a company and not from the market generally.

Statement of movements in reserves. A statement showing how each category of reserves (e.g., share premium, revaluation reserve) has changed during a financial year.

Statement of total recognized gains and losses. Statement bringing together those gains (e.g., profit for the year) and losses which have passed through the PROFIT AND LOSS ACCOUNT and those which have not (e.g., unrealized gain on revaluation of properties).

Statements of recommended practice (SORPs). Non-mandatory statements of accounting practice.

Statements of standard accounting practice (SSAPs). Statements of methods of accounting prepared by the former ACCOUNTING STANDARDS COMMITTEE and approved by the councils of the major professional accountancy bodies. Extant SSAPs have been adopted by the ACCOUNTING STANDARDS BOARD and apply to all financial statements intended to give a true and fair view.

Statutory accounts. Financial statements prepared in accordance with the Companies Act for filing with the REGISTRAR OF COMPANIES.

Stock exchange. A market where shares, debentures, government securities, etc., are bought and sold.

Stocks and work in progress. Comprises goods or other assets purchased for resale; consumable stores; raw materials and components; products and services in intermediate stages of completion; and finished goods. Valued at the lower of cost (HISTORICAL COST under historical cost accounting, REPLACEMENT COST under current cost accounting) or NET REALIZABLE VALUE.

Stock turnover. Ratio of sales (sometimes, cost of sales) to stock-in-trade.

Straight-line depreciation. Method of depreciation in which the periodic depreciation charge is obtained by dividing the cost less estimated scrap value of an asset by its estimated economic life.

Subdivision of share capital. Splitting of shares into smaller units (e.g., splitting one £1 share into two shares each valued at 50 p).

Subsidiary undertaking. An undertaking that is controlled by a PARENT UNDERTAKING. Its financial statements must be included in the GROUP ACCOUNTS unless the subsidiary is lawfully excluded from consolidation.

Substance over form. An accounting concept whereby transactions or other events are accounted for and presented in accordance with their economic substance rather than their legal form.

Summary financial statements. Financial statements permitted to be sent to the shareholders of listed companies summarizing the information contained in the annual accounts and directors' report. The latter need be sent only to shareholders who state that they wish to receive them. The form of the summary financial statements is prescribed.

Supplementary financial statements. Statements presented as additional to primary FINANCIAL STATEMENTS and explicitly or implicitly of less importance, e.g., historical cost statements can be supplemented by current cost statements.

Systematic (market) risk. Risk arising from the market, not from specific factors applicable to a company. Quantified as the BETA of a company's ORDINARY SHARES.

Table A. A model set of ARTICLES OF ASSOCIATION, which can be adopted by a company in full or in a modified form.

Take-over bid. An offer to purchase all, or a controlling percentage of, the share capital of a company.

Tangible fixed assets. Assets such as land and buildings, plant and machinery, and fixtures and fittings.

Taxable income. Income liable to tax. Not usually equal to the profit reported in a company's financial statements.

Tax credit. A credit received by shareholders at the same time as a dividend. Its amount is related to the rate of income tax. It can be set off against the liability to income tax on the dividend plus tax credit.

Times interest earned. The number of times that a company's interest is covered or earned by its profit before interest and tax.

Trade credit. Short-term source of funds resulting from credit granted by suppliers of goods bought.

Trade discount. A discount off the list price of a good. Sales and purchases are recorded net of trade discounts.

Trade mark. A distinctive identification, protected by law, of a manufactured product or of a service. An INTANGIBLE FIXED ASSET.

Trading on the equity. Using fixed-interest sources of capital to boost the return on the equity (ordinary shares).

True and fair view. The overriding reporting requirement for companies. The phrase is undefined but depends upon both the application of legal requirements and APPLICABLE ACCOUNTING STANDARDS and the exercise of judgement. If FINANCIAL STATEMENTS and the notes thereto do not in themselves give a true and fair view, additional information must be provided. In special circumstances the express requirements of the law and standards must be departed from if this is necessary in order to give a true and fair view. *A* true and fair view is required, not *the* true and fair view.

Turnover. Sales, i.e., the amounts derived from the provision of goods and services falling within a company's ordinary activities after deduction of trade discounts, VAT and similar taxes. In consolidated financial statements it excludes inter-company transactions. *See also* SEGMENT REPORTING.

Ultra vires. Latin for 'beyond the powers'. Especially applied to acts of a company not authorized by the objects clause of its MEMORANDUM OF ASSOCIATION.

Undistributable reserves. The aggregate of: share premium account; capital redemption reserve; accumulated unrealized profits, so far as not previously capitalized, *less* accumulated, unrealized losses, so far as not previously written off in a reduction or reorganization of capital; and other reserves which a company is prohibited from distributing.

Unit trust. Undertaking formed to invest in securities (mainly ordinary shares) under the terms of a trust deed. Not a company. Compare INVESTMENT TRUST.

Unlimited company. A COMPANY the liability of whose members is limited neither by shares nor by guarantee.

Unlisted investments. Investments which are not listed on a recognized British stock exchange or on any reputable stock exchange outside Great Britain. If they consist of equity of other companies, directors must give either an estimate of their value or information about income received, profits, etc.

Unlisted securities market (USM). A separate market for companies not large enough to be listed upon the stock exchange. It imposes less stringent regulations.

Unsecured loan. Money borrowed by a company without the giving of security.

Urgent Issues Task Force (UITF). A body which assists the ACCOUNTING STANDARDS BOARD in areas where an accounting standard or legal requirement exists, but where unsatisfactory or conflicting interpretations have developed or seem likely to develop. The UITF seeks to reach a consensus to which companies are expected to conform.

Value added statement. A statement showing for a period the wealth created (value added) by the operations of an enterprise and how the wealth has been distributed among employees, government, providers of capital, and replacement and expansion.

Value added tax (VAT). A tax based on the value added as goods pass from supplier of raw materials, to manufacturer, to wholesaler, to retailer, to consumer. Tax receivable can be set off against tax payable. Turnover is shown net of VAT in published profit and loss accounts.

Value to the business. The deprival value of an asset, i.e., the lower of its current replacement cost and RECOVERABLE AMOUNT. The basis of valuation in current cost accounting.

Variable overheads. Overheads which vary proportionately with manufacturing activity.

Window-dressing. The manipulation of figures in financial statements so as to produce a desired appearance and ratios on the balance sheet date.

Working capital. Current assets *less* current liabilities.

Work-in-progress. Partly completed manufactured goods.

Writing-down allowance. The annual amount deductible for tax purposes on certain TANGIBLE FIXED ASSETS.

Written-down value. The value of an asset in the books of a company or for tax purposes after depreciation has been written off.

Yield. The rate of return relating cash invested to cash received (or expected to be received).

Z-score. A measure of the SOLVENCY of a company calculated from an equation incorporating more than one FINANCIAL RATIO.

Appendix C. Annual Report and Accounts of British Vita PLC for the Year Ended 31 December 1992

Contents

Financial Highlights

£000	1992	1991
Turnover	**788,528**	694,276
United Kingdom	**14,727**	15,921
Continental Europe	**33,340**	35,742
International	**624**	1,675
Operating profit	**48,691**	53,338
Share of profits of associated undertakings	**5,623**	1,624
Profit on ordinary activities before interest	**54,314**	54,962
Interest	**842**	(4,606)
Profit on ordinary activities before tax	**55,156**	50,356
Return on average shareholders' funds	**22%**	31%
Earnings per share	**16.3p**	16.3p*
Dividend per share	**7.15p**	6.84p*

(* Adjusted for the 1992 Rights Issue)

Vita is an International leader in the application of science, technology and engineering .... to the production of specialised polymer, fibre and fabric components .... for the furnishing, transportation, apparel, packaging and engineering industries.

Chairman's Review

I am very pleased to be able to report that the overall results for the year show a most creditable achievement of almost 10% increase in profits to a record £55.2m. Earnings per share have been maintained at 16.3p, notwithstanding the increased number of shares arising from our March 1992 Rights Issue. The performance in the past year and, in particular, the profit achieved was influenced by a wide range of economic factors, currency fluctuations and, of course, the interest received on the Rights Issue funds.

In countering the problems of variable conditions in many of the markets in which we operate, we again have demonstrated the advantages of our spread of markets and products which give a degree of resilience to our overall performance, particularly during the turbulent times which exist at present. The withdrawal of the UK and Italy from the ERM and the major realignment of these and other European currencies caused some difficulties, mainly on the cost of imports, but we have seized and made the most of the opportunities for exports and import substitution in the territories affected.

In the UK, despite official outpourings, there are only a few signs that the end to the recession is, in reality, any nearer. The reduction in interest rates is a welcome contribution to optimism for industry although the increasing level of unemployment is still a worrying feature. Against this backcloth our results in the UK must be viewed as commendable. They reflect the benefit of improvements in manufacturing and quality systems and innovative product developments that provide the ability for our companies to keep in the forefront of their individual product and market sectors.

In Continental Europe we have, through most of last year, enjoyed reasonable conditions for trade and good progress was achieved especially in the foam and consumer product operations in the Netherlands, Germany and France. Towards the end of the year some deterioration of trading conditions became apparent in certain markets, particularly in the automotive and industrial sectors. Overall, the results in Europe were satisfactory especially as they were affected by losses in Spain where conditions generally worsened. Whilst determined management actions to improve this situation continued during the year with increasing intensity, the structure of industry, reducing automotive output and an overall weak state of trade unfortunately neutralised our efforts. Further rationalisation and consideration of alternative strategies within Spain will be a priority for 1993.

In our International operations, the profitability of our Zimbabwean subsidiary was severely affected by the drought which has now ended. In North America I am pleased to report that the results of Spartech, following its financial restructure and further quality and capital investment programmes, are now improving. Further progress is also being made in our foam activities in the USA, particularly in terms of market penetration and manufacturing efficiency.

The pursuit of growth continues to be the main objective of our strategy. During the year our programmes to achieve this by the twin routes of organic development and acquisition were followed. Almost £33m was invested in capital programmes and a few modest acquisitions were made, being mainly strategic additions to existing operations adding strength in the Swedish and Netherlands markets.

We have also expanded our horizons, both eastwards and westwards. In Poland we have formed a subsidiary and commenced work on a new factory to house a foam manufacture and conversion unit as well as, separately, going into a joint venture there in foam converting. We see these developments as a natural progression from our German operations but they will also enable us to fulfil part of the huge potential demand of markets in the East European countries. Moving westwards, early in 1993 we have added another unit to strengthen our foam operations in the USA, added to the Vita presence in Canada and Spartech has acquired business and assets to broaden its product range.

The search for compatible acquisitions continues and dozens of possibilities, both large and small, have been vetted but until the right opportunities at sensible prices are identified, the bulk of the

Rights Issue monies raised earlier in the year will remain untouched.

Throughout the year pressure on the management of working capital has been successfully applied. The Rights Issue proceeds remain available, resulting in an extremely strong balance sheet, with cash on hand exceeding borrowings by £43m.

At the end of this month, Mr David Hine is retiring and I wish to pay tribute to his contribution to Vita over almost 25 years, the last 14 years as a Main Board director especially concerned with our foam operations worldwide. The presentation to him last year of the Medal of Merit by the Urethane Group of the Plastics and Rubber Institute was a fitting and well deserved acknowledgement of his outstanding service to the polyurethane industry.

I would like to thank all our employees for their efforts and believe they can be proud of their achievements during the year. I know there is no risk of complacency and they will do everything possible to ensure our continued success in the challenging times ahead.

Amongst our primary objectives for this year will be to continue to seek growth both organically and by suitable acquisitions, further rigorous control of costs, continued investments in efficiency and to make positive inroads into specific problem areas. Indications of trading conditions in certain markets point to the first half of 1993 being a difficult environment in which to operate. Sales to date are slightly ahead of the same period last year but there is increasing pressure on margins due to tighter conditions being felt in some markets. However, we shall continue in the traditional Vita style of vigorous activity and service in the market place using all the advantages of market and technical leadership.

9 March 1993

R. McGee

Summary of Financial Data 1988 - 1992

Profit and Loss Account

£000

	1988	1989	1990	1991	1992
Turnover					
Company and subsidiaries' turnover	452,652	589,605	635,948	694,276	788,528
Share of associated undertakings' turnover	56,024	66,232	85,416	75,890	83,645
	508,676	655,837	721,364	770,166	872,173
Operating profit					
United Kingdom	13,462	14,951	16,591	15,921	14,727
Continental Europe	18,563	27,072	34,327	35,742	33,340
International	1,563	1,431	5,490	1,675	624
	33,588	43,454	56,408	53,338	48,691
Share of profits of associated undertakings	4,094	5,353	4,468	1,624	5,623
Profit before interest	37,682	48,807	60,876	54,962	54,314
Interest receivable (payable)	(159)	(1,171)	(3,192)	(4,606)	842
Profit on ordinary activities before taxation	37,523	47,636	57,684	50,356	55,156
Taxation	(14,830)	(17,841)	(22,497)	(20,322)	(21,216)
Profit on ordinary activities after taxation	22,693	29,795	35,187	30,034	33,940
Minority interests	(205)	(273)	(321)	(332)	(395)
Profit for the financial year	22,488	29,522	34,866	29,702	33,545
Dividends	(7,350)	(10,203)	(11,724)	(12,476)	(15,296)
Retained profit for the financial year	15,138	19,319	23,142	17,226	18,249

The prior year figures have been presented in compliance with Financial Reporting Standard 3.

Turnover by class of business

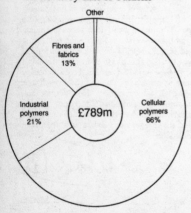

Turnover by geographical destination

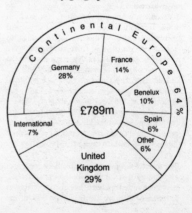

Balance Sheet

£000

	1988	1989	1990	1991	1992
Net assets					
Tangible fixed assets	115,306	148,824	164,504	184,277	**218,022**
Investments	11,296	23,115	17,404	16,874	**20,101**
Net current assets	34,683	20,354	30,021	21,301	**100,154**
Creditors falling due after more than one year	(28,512)	(33,106)	(38,544)	(29,934)	**(31,528)**
Provisions for liabilities and charges	(11,560)	(16,770)	(18,618)	(18,889)	**(22,183)**
Minority interests	(1,049)	(1,654)	(1,164)	(1,360)	**(2,991)**
	120,164	140,763	153,603	172,269	**281,575**
Ratios					
Operating profit as a percentage of					
Company and subsidiaries' turnover	7.4%	7.4%	8.9%	7.7%	**6.2%**
Return on average shareholders' funds†	34%	37%	39%	31%	**22%**
Gearing (net cash)	7%	21%	17%	20%	**(15%)**
Earnings per share previously reported†	13.0	16.8	18.2	16.3	**-**
Earnings per share FRS 3 adjusted	13.0	16.6	19.4	16.3	**16.3**
Dividend per share†	4.19p	5.69p	6.50p	6.84p	**7.15p**
Number of times covered	3.1	2.9	3.0	2.4	**2.2**
Net assets per share†	69p	79p	85p	94p	**132p**
Number of shares in issue†	170.2m	173.7m	175.0m	177.1m	**213.9m**
Average number of shares in issue†	173.6m	177.2m	179.8m	181.7m	**206.4m**

† Adjusted for the 1988 and 1990 capitalisation and 1992 rights issues, as appropriate.

The prior year figures, ratios and graphs have been presented in compliance with Financial Reporting Standard 3.

Source and growth of profits
(before interest)

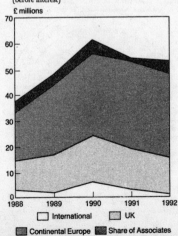

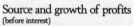

Earnings and dividends

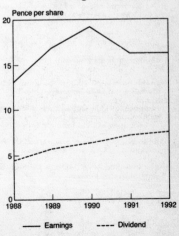

Directors and Officers

Chairman	R. McGee FIM, CIMgt, FRSA
Deputy chairman	L. D. Lawton OBE, DL, BA, FRSA (non-executive)
Chief executive	R. H. Sellers BSc(Econ), FCA, DpBa, CIMgt
Deputy chief executive	F. J. Eaton FIM
Directors	K. R. Bhatt BCom, MCT
	D. R. Hine BSc, CEng, MIChemE, AMCT
	J. H. Ogden (non - executive)
	F. A. Parker FCA, CIMgt, FRSA (non - executive)
Secretary	A. R. Teague FCCA
Corporate solicitor	M. R. Stirzaker BA

Robert McGee, 58, joined Vita in 1955. He was appointed to the Board in 1972, became Chief Executive in 1975 and succeeded Mr Parker as Chairman in 1988.

Rod Sellers, 46, joined Vita in 1971 and was appointed to the Board as Finance Director in 1974. He assumed the responsibilities of Chief Executive in 1990.

Kanak Bhatt, 53, joined Vita in October 1966 becoming Group Chief Accountant in 1976, Group Treasurer in 1986 and was appointed to the Board in 1991.

Fernley Parker, 73, retired after nearly 10 years as Chairman in 1987, having progressed with the Company as Secretary, Finance Director and Chief Executive since joining in 1954. He remains as Chairman of British Vita Pensions Trust Limited and is a member of the University Court of the University of Salford.

Duncan Lawton, 65, joined Vita in 1968, was appointed to the Board in 1972 and became Deputy Chairman in 1988. Mr Lawton is a Deputy Lieutenant of Greater Manchester, a National Council Member of the CBI and was awarded the OBE in 1989 for services to industry.

Frank Eaton, 53, joined Vita in 1958, was appointed to the Board in 1975 and became Deputy Chief Executive in 1991. He is a Council Member of RAPRA.

David Hine, 50, joined Vita in 1968 and was appointed to the Board in 1979. Mr Hine retires on 31 March 1993.

James Ogden, 71, has been closely associated with the Company since 1954, has been a non-executive Director since 1967 and is a Director of British Vita Pensions Trust Limited. Mr Ogden is a retired partner of a Manchester firm of solicitors.

Management Board members

Laurence Butterworth, 48, with 29 years experience in Vitafoam is Chairman of Vita's cellular foam companies in the UK.

Filiep Libeert, 39, heads the Continental European fibre operations, with companies in Germany and Sweden as well as his base at Libeltex in Belgium which has been part of Vita since 1979.

Jim Smethurst, 48, has 29 years experience in Vita's UK fibre and fabrics sectors and is chairman of those operations.

Frans Willems, 58, joined Vita 13 years ago and heads up the Dutch parent company, Vita Interfoam.

Dr. Joachim Grönebaum, 54, who joined Vita in 1985 with the acquisition of the Solvay foam interests, heads up Deutsche Vita's cellular foam interests throughout Germany.

Jim Mercer, 47, with almost 24 years experience in Vita's UK elastomeric and automotive component operations is responsible for the industrial polymer and engineering thermoplastics interests throughout the UK and Europe.

Philippe Vassort, 53, heads the cellular foam operations in France centred on Tramico which became a member of Vita in 1984.

Operations Review

This review of the operations of Vita is divided into sections corresponding with the financial analysis provided in note 1 to the accounts.

Cellular polymers

Operations within the cellular polymers sector, with a broad product range from block and converted foams, through specialised mouldings, composites and rebonded products, to foam mattresses and consumer products, generated turnover of £518m and an operating profit of £32.1m.

All the cellular polymer operations entered 1992 anticipating a difficult year with increasing competition and continuing pressure on margins. This proved to be the case as the year progressed but most operations achieved a high degree of success in meeting their objectives.

Since the realignment of sterling outside the ERM, all the UK businesses in the sector have had to cope with increased raw material costs and to recoup as much as possible with increased selling prices.

Apart from Spain, the European foam operations avoided most of the raw material pricing problems associated with the currency realignment but all suffered similar pressures on margins throughout the year. Competition remained strong everywhere but Vita operations all successfully defended their market share.

In the UK, Vitafoam maintained its volumes in a static market with inevitable reduction in margins, aggravated by the problems of actual and potential bad debts. In the latter part of the year, its continued commitment to product development culminated in the successful launch of the new 'Reflex' product, enabling continued full compliance with all existing fire regulations to be achieved from a foam manufactured without the addition of melamine. Furthermore, the new 'V' range of combustion modified ether foams with their improved characteristics have proved of

particular interest to the bedding and caravan markets and the additional range of qualities should enable Vitafoam to maintain its market leadership.

Development has continued on the new round-block production facilities and major capital expenditure has been invested in a new production unit, which should be commissioned in mid 1993, for the 'Vitec' range of impregnated specialist foam products.

Caligen Foam has been heavily involved in product development following the successful commissioning in late 1991 of its new foam plant, which is undoubtedly one of the most sophisticated in the world, and good progress has been made in the achievement of the anticipated improved efficiencies.

The exporting achievements of the UK automotive industry benefitted sales of peeled foam which contributed significantly to Caligen's performance. Improvement was achieved in the specialised, conversion, industrial and consumer product divisions.

Kay-Metzeler, with its wider industrial commercial base, did not benefit to the same extent from demand from the automotive sector but still achieved a very satisfactory result. A major project for the installation of new hot-cure moulded-foam facilities at Bollington was virtually completed by the year-end. Plans were implemented for the rationalisation, in early 1993, of similar outdated facilities at Middleton, with the additional environmental benefit of the elimination of the use of CFCs in moulding production.

Kay-Metzeler's block and conversion divisions continued to benefit from the development of a wider range of specialist foams for the packaging, medical and aircraft markets rather than duplicate the product range of its sister companies.

Ball & Young, as a newly integrated supplier of underlay and accessories to the floor-covering market, increased sales of underlay in a very competitive arena and successfully regained lost business, against severe competition, in the accessories sector.

Without growth in the market, the French operations achieved a most commendable result in line with expectations, with overall volumes being maintained in spite of increased competition. The Tramivex headliner product continued its worldwide acceptance. A new licence covering Argentina and Chile was granted to an Argentinean company and there was a resumption of royalty income from the USA from a new licensee. Development continues on both new markets and applications for the process. Tramico automotive sales fluctuated in line with the fortunes of its major French automotive manufacturers, but a better year in 1993 is anticipated as new models are launched. Benefits of the recent new foam plant installation continue, including increased productivity enabling market share to be maintained in the competitive environment.

The ICOA operation in France recovered well from the reduction in volume, early in the year, when a major customer installed in-house production.

The Netherlands operations experienced similar difficult market conditions, especially in the furniture trade, but transportation markets remained strong. Production facilities have recently been expanded to manufacture reticulated foam. Demand for the latex products of Radium continued to strengthen and the Radium operations are now mid-way through a major three year improvement and reorganisation programme. The acquisition in early 1992 of the Norma and Oost operations significantly enhanced the involvement of Vita in the Netherlands mattress market, although the post-acquisition rationalisation and integration necessary reduced the initial benefits in the year. Early in 1993, Oost relocated to new, larger, purpose-built facilities at Almere, near Amsterdam, and the marketing of the Vita

Dutch mattress operations is now being co-ordinated by the newly created Vidor parent company.

In Germany, demand remained generally high except for a downturn in transportation products in the last quarter. Most of the adverse implications of the subsequent reduction in production were countered by modest rationalisation and success in sourcing alternative product opportunities. Demand for consumer products exceeded plans, aided by continuing development of new applications, such as the 'Biotec' product illustrated.

At the major Memmingen site in southern Germany, a new short block store was commissioned to improve service to external furniture customers. At the Wega site a major modernisation of the conversion departments to improve productivity was started. The existing operation in the former East Germany showed substantial improvement and, in July 1992, a new conversion outstation was purchased at Gehren in Thuringia, for which the initial results are very encouraging.

Increasing trade has been undertaken with Eastern Europe and since the year-end protracted negotiations have been concluded by Vita Polymers Poland for the construction of a new purpose-built foam production facility during 1993 in Poland to help develop the potential of a growing market. In addition, the Veenendaal operation in Germany has entered into a joint venture with a local company in Poland to operate, from March 1993, a new foam conversion factory. These developments will help meet the increasing local demand for products as more customers relocate their production facilities in Eastern Europe.

In Spain, the ICOA operations experienced severe and increasing problems throughout the year with the foam sector suffering extreme competition because of over-capacity, low demand and raw material price increases. All these factors also adversely affected the automotive sector which accounts for most of the losses incurred. Throughout the year, progress has been made, albeit at substantial cost, with various rationalisation projects especially reducing numbers of personnel.

The International cellular polymer operations had mixed experiences with the profitability of the Zimbabwean subsidiary being severely affected by the drought and associated difficulties. The Vitafoam subsidiary in the USA has successfully established itself as a local producer in its first full year and has very recently added a further production unit with the acquisition of Nabors Manufacturing.

Industrial polymers

Operations within the industrial polymers sector, with a wide product range from rubber and plastics compounds in liquid or solid form through mouldings, coatings, extrusions and decorative laminate, to engineering thermoplastics supplied as sheet or vacuum formed, generated turnover of £163m and an operating profit of £7.6m.

The effects of the current economic climate have been most obvious in the industrial operations in the UK, Germany and Spain, which have had to cope with a very difficult situation.

In the UK, Vitamol achieved a satisfactory result from its various moulding operations, including the newly acquired business of PUPA Plastics, but future prospects remain difficult. Vitacom had an encouraging year with tangible benefits from past rationalisation aided by new machinery installations and the purchase during the year of the business of RE Rubber.

Vita Liquid Polymers achieved higher than planned sales despite the current depressed state of their traditional markets. Sales of specialist fire-retardant products increased well and the sister organisation, RLA Polymers in Australia, achieved an excellent result in the very difficult local economy.

Compared to the previous year when two sites manufacturing proofed fabrics were merged, Vita Industrial Polymers achieved a significant improvement in performance despite minimal volume increase as a result of improvements to productivity and cost control. Sales to the coal industry declined significantly in the year but continued attention to new product development in all areas proved worthwhile with, for example, Vitacel's expansion into sports equipment and equestrian protective clothing.

Thermoplastic operations at Royalite had mixed fortunes with continued depressed demand at all sites in the UK but strong trading at the Roon operations in France and Royalite in Italy. The main UK operation at Newbridge continued to develop more specialist products and reduce involvement in automotive sectors. The pressure forming operations at Livingston started the year quietly but demand for new tooling increased significantly towards the end of the year. The industrial sheet operations on the Wrexham site showed continued improvement with future benefits anticipated from the new line currently being commissioned.

The Roon operations experienced good demand but the forthcoming volume reduction, due to customer's respecification of certain lighting products, will mean a difficult task to maintain sales levels in the forthcoming year.

At Royalite Italy, the new production plant has enabled significant progress to be made in opening up new markets for caravan and sanitary ware products. Exports to Poland and Turkey increased, a trial order to China was fulfilled but further potential in Yugoslavia was frustrated by current hostilities.

The operations of Esbjerg Thermoplast in Denmark continued to benefit from strong links with major local sheet customers in the refrigeration and toy markets. After a disappointing first-half, fibre sales developed well, both as a result of increased export sales and improved production efficiencies from recent capital expenditure to increase capacity.

Metzeler Plastics in Germany experienced a reduction in demand towards the year-end after a very busy first-half but a major new wide-width production line commissioned late in the year opens up new markets. The laminate production, both in Germany where the business expanded into full production of laminated elements, and more significantly at Metzeler Laminados in Spain, continued to suffer from a decline in the market for current products. The new replacement melamine product was only slowly introduced as development and production trials of the new line in Spain were completed.

Fibres and fabrics

Operations within the fibres and fabrics sector, covering fibre processing across Europe and specialised fabric production and laminates in the UK, generated turnover of £105m and an operating profit of £6.4m.

The Vitafibres businesses performed well when considering their dependency on the UK market. The operations benefitted from closer co-operation with customers in developing products for more technical applications, for example the healthcare market. Export sales were maintained overall, with Alpha Flock in particular expanding further into Europe and Australia. Pennine Fibres have enjoyed a significant increase in demand since the devaluation of sterling, reflected in both exports and the substitution in the UK of more expensive imported fibre. The Bedcrest operations had a successful year for quilts and pillows whilst maintaining growth in medical bandage products.

In Belgium, the Libeltex fibre operations had another successful year, despite increasing competition and pressure on margins. Significant benefits accrued from ongoing product development and the further extension of the very successful Total Transaction Quality programme. Expansion into Sweden was

continued with the acquisition in early 1992 of Sporda and substantial progress made on the integration of the existing Lagans and Sporda operating units onto one site. Libeltex's subsidiary in Germany was slightly less successful, falling short of expectations due to reduced local demand.

The Vita-tex UK textile operations were less successful than in the recent past, especially at SA Driver where changing fashion lessened demand for some of the range of products manufactured. The S&T operation fared relatively well with improvements in specialist products more than offsetting the decline in more basic items. At Woodeaves significant improvements were made in productivity and increased sales were obtained for upholstery fabrics, mainly to Continental Europe.

The Rossendale Combining business achieved increased sales volumes in both flame and adhesive lamination sectors, again obtaining major benefits from the development of specialist products in close co-operation with customers. The Denbilaminates operations showed improvement on the previous year, although margins and competition remain extremely difficult.

Corporate and other

Operations within this sector, comprising parent and service companies within the corporate structure, together with the UK property and Swiss licensing operations, generated an operating profit of £2.6m.

In addition to overall strategic development, certain key or specialised services continue to be provided by the Corporate Centre team, including the co-ordination of policy on quality, product development and environmental issues.

The success of the Quality Awareness programme is clearly represented by the large number of Vita's operations throughout the world which have successfully achieved and retained BS5750 or ISO9002 recognition. Seven more companies achieved the highly regarded accreditation in 1992 and several more companies which are not yet accredited are well advanced with the necessary preparations. The Quality programme also aims to minimise the quantity of process waste, much of which is immediately re-processed. Innovative uses are being developed to recycle customers' offcuts and pre-consumer waste into new materials.

Vita companies operating in similar fields participate in product development and technical liaison groups sharing ideas and developing solutions to our own and customers' product requirements.

New legislation is being adopted throughout the world to protect the environment and Vita companies continue to prioritise compliance, general improvement and awareness programmes. For example, Vita is rapidly reducing the use of CFCs in the production of cellular polymers well before the relevant deadlines imposed, with several companies having already discontinued their use, including in Germany where CFCs are now banned by legislation.

The Centre Treasury team has been responsible for optimising the investment return on the funds raised by the March 1992 Rights Issue until suitable acquisitions are identified, together with assistance in managing the effects of the significant currency fluctuations in 1992.

Associates

Vita's investment in associated undertakings has generated £5.6m contribution to Group results from a share of turnover of £84m.

The cellular polymer operations in Canada achieved a good result. From 1 January 1993, operations were expanded by the purchase, by Vitafoam Products Canada, of Pre Fab Cushioning Products. Pre Fab is one of Vita's major and oldest Canadian customers and operates a foam conversion factory in Toronto. A good performance has again been achieved, in local currency terms, from the operations in Nigeria and the companies in Egypt and Ireland also had a successful year.

Spartech, the engineered thermoplastic company in the USA, enjoyed a significant improvement in profitability, partially as a result of the financial restructuring undertaken during the year. A new extrusion line at the Missouri rigid sheet operation increased capacity and a new clean room facility at the Californian operation provides the opportunity to develop new products for the food and medical packaging markets. In January 1993, Spartech purchased part of the extrusion business of Penda Corporation which should increase annual rigid sheet rollstock sales by up to US$15m.

In the UK, BTR-Vitaline achieved a very satisfactory result, despite the generally low level of activity in the chemical industry.

After an extremely successful start to the year, the operations of Vita-Achter slowed down in the last quarter as a direct result of reduced demand from a major customer. However, its widening customer and product base, plus proven organisational and quality systems which have enabled direct textile exports to Japanese automotive manufacturers in Japan, means the business is well established for the longer term.

The directors have pleasure in presenting their annual report and accounts for the year ended 31 December 1992.

Profits and dividends

The profit for the financial year ended 31 December 1992 is £33,545,00 in the Group and £18,509,000 in the Company, before provision for dividends, paid and proposed, of £15,296,000. Retained profit for the financial year of £18,249,000 has been transferred to reserves.

An interim dividend of 3.5p per Ordinary share was paid on 9 November 1992. The directors now propose a final dividend of 3.65p per Ordinary share payable on 10 May 1993 to shareholders on the Register at 8 April 1993 making a total Ordinary dividend for the year of 7.15p (net) per share (6.84p (net) after adjustment for the 1992 Rights Issue)

Principal activities

Vita is principally concerned with the manufacture and processing of polymers, including cellular foams, synthetic fibre fillings, specialised and coated textiles, polymeric compounds and mouldings and engineering thermoplastics. It also has interests in the licensing of advanced technical processes.

The principal operations are reviewed on pages 8 to 16, which form part of this directors' report.

Fixed assets

Excluding the investment in new subsidiary undertakings, expenditure by the Group on tangible fixed assets during the year, including those of businesses acquired on an assets basis, was £32,785,000, compared to £33,554,000 in 1991. Details of some of the major investments are provided in the Operations Review and the financial details are given in note 11.

In accordance with the Group policy of four-yearly revaluations, the results of the land and building revaluation undertaken as at the end of the year have been included in these accounts, as detailed in note 11.

Subsidiary and associated undertakings

During the year, Vita has continued to make modest but strategic acquisitions commencing, as detailed in last year's report and accounts, in January 1992 with the acquisition by Libeltex NV of 70% of the issued share capital of Sporda Vadd Forsalyning AB with its fibre processing facilities at Bredaryd and Lidhult in Sweden. Also in January 1992, Vita Interfoam BV acquired the entire issued share capital of Norma Boxmeer BV, a manufacturer of mattresses from premises near Eindhoven.

As part of the financial restructuring of Spartech, Vita subscribed, in April 1992, for an additional 750,000 shares of Common Stock at US$2 each. Following the completed restructuring Vita's interest in the Common Stock of Spartech reduced from 29% to 24%.

Also in April, Vita Interfoam BV acquired the issued share capital of Ledikanten-en Matrassen Fabriek Oost BV, together with its subsidiary Sanaform BV, to further expand Vita's share of the Netherlands foam mattress market. Currently, these new interests, together with existing operations in the same market, are being restructured under a new holding company, Vidor BV.

In June 1992, Vita formed a new subsidiary company, Vita Polymers Poland Sp.zo.o, to spearhead expansion into Eastern Europe. Many months of preparatory work culminated in the December announcement that Vita had undertaken an initial investment of £4m to build a foam production and conversion plant on land acquired near Wroclaw in Poland.

Directors' Report (continued)

In July 1992, a small foam conversion unit at Gehren in the Thuringia region of Germany was acquired.

In September, Vita's shareholding in Isofel SA was increased by 19.5% to 67.5%, changing the status of this Spanish supplier to the automotive industry from associate to subsidiary.

With effect from 1 January 1993, Vita associate Vitafoam Products Canada Limited acquired the assets and business of one of its major and oldest customers, Pre Fab Cushioning Products, which operates a foam conversion business in Toronto.

In February 1993, Vitafoam Inc. in the US acquired the assets and goodwill of Nabors Manufacturing Co. of Chattanooga, Tennessee to extend its operations in the USA.

The Group's principal subsidiary and associated undertakings are listed on pages 42 to 44 of this report and accounts.

Corporate governance

Following the publication of the Report of the Committee on the Financial Aspects of Corporate Governance (the Cadbury Report), the directors have reviewed their compliance with the Code of Best Practice.

Vita is managed by a Main Board, consisting of executive and non-executive members, who retain responsibility for the formulation of corporate strategy, approval of acquisitions and major capital expenditure and treasury policy. Control of operational matters is delegated to a Management Board, comprising the executive directors and seven chairmen or managing directors of UK and European subsidiaries. The membership of both Boards by the executive directors thus ensures a strong link between the strategy and the implementation and both Boards

meet regularly to monitor performance and co-ordinate overall policy.

Members of both Boards, who have all served throughout the year, are listed on page 6 of this report and accounts.

The Chairman and all non-executive directors constitute a Remuneration Committee to advise on both Board and senior staff remuneration policy. The non-executive directors also form an Audit Committee, chaired by Mr Parker, to review the half-year and annual financial statements and matters related to both the external audit and internal audit function.

The directors believe that, having made minor modifications to formalise existing procedures, Vita now substantially complies with the Code of Best Practice, as far as is currently possible.

Mr D.R. Hine has notified the Company of his intention to take early retirement, and to resign as a director of the Company on 31 March 1993 when his current service contract expires. The Board of Vita acknowledges the excellent contribution made by Mr Hine to the development of Vita during his 25 years of service and, in particular, his services as a director since 1979.

Mr L.D. Lawton relinquished his executive duties at the end of June 1992 and was appointed a non-executive director with a fixed term service contract until January 1994, subject to his re-election by shareholders. In accordance with the Articles of Association, Mr Lawton retires as a non-executive director, by rotation, at the conclusion of the forthcoming Annual General Meeting, and, being eligible, offers himself for re-appointment. Accordingly, Resolution 3 of the Notice of Meeting will be proposed.

Mr J.H. Ogden and Mr F.A. Parker have both attained the age of 70 and their re-appointment as non-executive directors requires the specific approval of shareholders, in accordance with Section 293 (5) of the Companies Act 1985. Accordingly, Resolutions 4 and 5 of the Notice of Meeting will be proposed. As their appointment requires annual re-approval, Mr Ogden and Mr Parker do not have service contracts.

The Company purchases insurance cover to protect directors and officers against liability for negligence.

Directors' and other interests

The interests of the directors in the Ordinary share capital of the Company as at 31 December 1992 is given below and details of the directors' interest in share options is given in note 9 to the accounts.

Shareholdings:

31 December 1992

	Beneficial	Non-beneficial	Options
R. McGee	662,867	90,000	9,834
L.D. Lawton	510,123	102,245	-
R.H. Sellers	350,726	521,266	113,475
F.J. Eaton	469,396	-	80,950
K.R. Bhatt	132,728	-	98,702
D.R. Hine	354,806	-	8,568
J.H. Ogden	80,235	2,629,682	-
F.A. Parker	3,537,249	1,435,673	-

31 December 1991

	Beneficial	Non-beneficial	Options
R. McGee	712,527	90,000	8,075
L.D. Lawton	595,615	100,000	-
R.H. Sellers	371,502	1,006,266	111,149
F.J. Eaton	465,380	-	80,071
K.R. Bhatt	129,338	-	70,436
D.R. Hine	347,059	-	151,639
J.H. Ogden	80,235	3,225,582	-
F.A. Parker	3,537,249	2,035,673	-

Prior year option figures have been restated as a result of the 1992 Rights Issue.

Duplications in the table of non-beneficial interests amount to 1,856,939 (2,966,939) Ordinary shares. In addition to the above table, British Vita Pensions Trust Limited, of which four of the directors of the Company are also directors, holds 1,960,692 (2,710,692) Ordinary shares. Mr J.H. Ogden also has a non-beneficial interest in 5,320 (5,320) British Vita Preference shares.

There has been no change in the directors' interests between 31 December 1992 and 8 March 1993.

The Prudential Corporation group of companies has an interest in 5.23% of the issued share capital of the Company.

Apart from the disclosures above, the directors are not aware of any other interest in excess of 3%.

The Company is not a close company within the provisions of the Income and Corporation Taxes Act 1970.

Directors' Report (continued)

Throughout the year no director had any significant interest in any contract or arrangement entered into by the Company or its subsidiary or associated undertakings.

Share capital

On 4 March 1992, the Board announced a 1 for 5 Rights Issue which resulted in the allotment and issue of an additional 35,416,471 Ordinary shares at a price of 212p.

Shareholders approved, at the last Annual General Meeting, an increase in the Authorised Ordinary Share Capital to £75m by the creation of an additional 60m Ordinary shares of 25p each.

During the year, 1,353,649 Ordinary shares were issued and allotted, fully paid, under the employee share option schemes and 80,609 shares were issued and allotted, fully paid, in response to applications in accordance with the rules of the Vita PEPs. The annual costs of administering the PEPs are met by the Company and 283 (137) individual PEP accounts had been opened by the end of December 1992, controlling 592,831 (372,688) Ordinary shares in the Company.

At the end of the year, 213,926,954 Ordinary shares were in issue and by 8 March 1993 the number had increased to 213,978,796 through the issue of 40,628 shares in accordance with the rules of the share option schemes and 11,214 shares in accordance with the rules of the Vita PEPs.

The Companies Act 1985 requires that any equity securities issued wholly for cash must be offered to existing shareholders in proportion to their existing holdings, although this requirement may be disapplied by resolution of the shareholders. Such a disapplication is necessary so as to overcome the practical difficulties that arise on a rights issue and also to permit issues for cash otherwise than by way of rights to a limited extent.

To this end, a special resolution was passed at the Annual General Meeting in April 1992 expiring on the date of the forthcoming Annual General Meeting. Accordingly, Resolution 7 will be proposed as a special resolution at the Annual General Meeting to renew this authority for the directors to allot equity securities for cash as if the pre-emption rights contained in the Companies Act 1985 did not apply. In the case of allotments other than for rights issues, the authority is limited to shares representing 2.5% of the Authorised Ordinary share capital of the Company. This authority is sought for a further year with the intention of seeking renewal annually.

Personnel

The employees of Vita have long been regarded as one of its most important assets. The nature of the decentralised management structure creates many smaller operating units which promotes a greater sense of involvement by personnel in the success and development of 'their' business. The regular circulation of the employee newspaper 'Vitanews' ensures that all employees are kept informed of acquisitions and developments throughout the entire worldwide organisation and the Vita magazine, although primarily aimed at the external audience of shareholders and other interested parties, is also made available to employees. Both publications carry extracts from the Annual Report and Accounts and the Interim Report, even though copies of both documents are also made available to all employees.

Employee involvement in the overall performance of Vita has been encouraged by promoting participation in the employee share option schemes since the first scheme was established in 1974. An approved savings related scheme was created in 1981 and renewed, with Inland Revenue and shareholders approval, in 1991 and a similar scheme was created in 1990 to extend the benefits to international employees. An executive share option scheme has also operated since 1984 and the extent of employee participation in the individual schemes is detailed in note 19 to the accounts.

Well - established consultative committee arrangements are actively maintained, together with collective bargaining procedures with recognised Trade Unions. Procedures are also well established to safeguard the health and safety of employees and ensure compliance with appropriate legislation.

Vita operates a totally non - discriminatory employment policy, part of which is the proper consideration of all applications for employment from disabled persons. Those who are appointed together with any disabled during employment receive, with their able - bodied colleagues, training for career development and promotion, consistent with their own abilities and the needs of their employing company.

The Board is very aware of both the commercial and social importance of training its employees and utilises an increasingly wide variety of internal and external facilities to improve the effectiveness with which staff, at all levels, undertake their duties.

In the UK, Vita Services Limited is registered as an Approved Training Organisation and acts as a Managing Agent for Career and Skills Training, providing up to 170 high quality training places to young or unemployed persons working towards recognised National Vocational qualifications or their equivalents. The Company remains supportive of the objectives of Training Enterprise Councils to improve the quality and relevance of training and for the last three years Mr L.D. Lawton has been Chairman of the Rochdale T.E.C.

Donations

A political donation of £10,000 was made to the Conservative Party and charitable donations made during the year amounted to £71,717.

Auditors

A resolution proposing the re-appointment of Arthur Andersen as auditors of the Company will be put to the Annual General Meeting.

By order of the Board

A.R. Teague

9 March 1993   *Secretary*

Consolidated Profit and Loss Account

for the year ended 31 December 1992

| | | | 1992 | | |
| | | | | | £000 |

	Notes	Continuing operations	Acquisitions	Total	1991
Turnover	1	**768,015**	**20,513**	**788,528**	694,276
Cost of sales		**(586,627)**	**(16,071)**	**(602,698)**	(527,600)
Gross profit		**181,388**	**4,442**	**185,830**	166,676
Distribution costs		**(47,288)**	**(1,022)**	**(48,310)**	(41,575)
Administrative expenses		**(86,196)**	**(2,633)**	**(88,829)**	(71,763)
Operating profit	2	**47,904**	**787**	**48,691**	53,338
Share of profits of associated undertakings	3	**5,623**	-	**5,623**	1,624
Profit on ordinary activities before interest		**53,527**	**787**	**54,314**	54,962
Interest receivable (payable)	4			**842**	(4,606)
Profit on ordinary activities before taxation				**55,156**	50,356
Tax on profit on ordinary activities	5			**(21,216)**	(20,322)
Profit on ordinary activities after taxation				**33,940**	30,034
Minority interests				**(395)**	(332)
Profit for the financial year				**33,545**	29,702
Dividends	6			**(15,296)**	(12,476)
Retained profit for the financial year	20			**18,249**	17,226
Retained by					
The Company				**3,213**	533
Subsidiary undertakings				**12,590**	18,070
Associated undertakings				**2,446**	(1,377)
				18,249	17,226
Earnings per ordinary share	7			**16.3 p**	16.3 p*

* Restated as a result of the 1992 Rights Issue.

The statement of movement in reserves is given in note 20.

Notes on pages 26 to 44 form part of these accounts.

	Notes	1992	1991
			£000

Statement of total recognised gains and losses

	Notes	1992	1991
Profit for the financial year		33,545	29,702
Unrealised surplus on revaluation of properties	20	5,231	-
		38,776	29,702
Currency translation differences on foreign currency net investments	20	15,704	(185)
Total recognised gains relating to the year		54,480	29,517

Note of historical cost profits and losses

	Notes	1992	1991
Reported profit on ordinary activities before taxation		55,156	50,356
Realised property revaluation gains of previous years	20	81	24
Actual depreciation charge		2,644	2,585
Historical cost depreciation charge		(2,435)	(2,255)
Historical cost profit on ordinary activities before taxation		55,446	50,710
Taxation	5	(21,216)	(20,322)
Minority interests		(395)	(332)
Dividends	6	(15,296)	(12,476)
Historical cost profit for the financial year retained		18,539	17,580

Reconciliation of movements in shareholders' funds

	Notes	1992	1991
Profit for the financial year		33,545	29,702
Dividends	6	(15,296)	(12,476)
		18,249	17,226
Other recognised gains (losses) relating to the year (net)		20,935	(185)
New share capital subscribed	24	75,167	1,737
Goodwill written-off	12	(5,045)	(112)
Net addition to shareholders' funds		109,306	18,666
Opening shareholders' funds		172,269	153,603
Closing shareholders' funds		281,575	172,269

The movement in the shareholders' funds of the Company from £83,250,000 to £161,630,000 comprises retained profit for the financial year of £3,213,000 and new share capital subscribed of £75,167,000. There is no difference between profit for the financial year and total recognised gains and historical cost profit for the Company.

Notes on pages 26 to 44 form part of these accounts.

Balance Sheets

as at 31 December 1992

£000

	Notes	Group 1992	Group 1991	Company 1992	Company 1991
Fixed assets					
Tangible assets	11	**218,022**	184,277	**96**	82
Investments	12	**20,101**	16,874	**91,726**	87,031
		238,123	201,151	**91,822**	87,113
Current assets					
Stocks	13	**67,678**	59,491	**-**	-
Debtors falling due within one year	14	**140,674**	126,764	**22,120**	10,059
Debtors falling due after more than one year	14	**592**	491	**2,012**	2,125
Cash at bank and short term investments		**101,248**	45,768	**71,884**	10,909
		310,192	232,514	**96,016**	23,093
Creditors: amounts falling due within one year					
Borrowings	15	**(28,955)**	(52,133)	**(2,291)**	(3,454)
Others	15	**(181,083)**	(159,080)	**(13,099)**	(9,640)
		(210,038)	(211,213)	**(15,390)**	(13,094)
Net current assets		**100,154**	21,301	**80,626**	9,999
Total assets less current liabilities		**338,277**	222,452	**172,448**	97,112
Creditors: amounts falling due after more than one year					
Borrowings	16	**(29,291)**	(27,795)	**(8,088)**	(10,984)
Others	16	**(2,237)**	(2,139)	**(2,548)**	(2,546)
		(31,528)	(29,934)	**(10,636)**	(13,530)
Provisions for liabilities and charges	18	**(22,183)**	(18,889)	**(182)**	(332)
		284,566	173,629	**161,630**	83,250
Capital and reserves					
Called up share capital	19	**53,539**	44,327	**53,539**	44,327
Share premium account	20	**81,228**	15,273	**81,228**	15,273
Revaluation reserve	20	**17,417**	11,912	**-**	-
Other reserves	20	**3,646**	3,034	**9,440**	9,440
Profit and loss account	20	**125,745**	97,723	**17,423**	14,210
		281,575	172,269	**161,630**	83,250
Minority interests		**2,991**	1,360	**-**	-
		284,566	173,629	**161,630**	83,250

The accounts on pages 22 to 44 were approved by the Board on 9 March 1993 and were signed on its behalf by:

R. McGee
K.R. Bhatt   Directors

Notes on pages 26 to 44 form part of these accounts.

(170)

Cash Flow Statement

for the year ended 31 December 1992

£000

	1992		1991
Net cash inflow from operating activities (note 22)		71,151	69,457
Returns on investments and servicing of finance			
Interest received	7,556		6,131
Interest paid	(6,689)		(10,506)
Interest element of finance lease rental payments	(250)		(231)
Dividends received from associated undertakings	1,592		1,638
Dividends paid to minority interests	(190)		(153)
Dividends paid	(13,860)		(12,056)
Net cash outflow from returns on investments and servicing of finance		(11,841)	(15,177)
Taxation			
UK corporation tax paid	(3,475)		(6,153)
Overseas tax paid	(12,481)		(13,845)
Tax paid		(15,956)	(19,998)
Investing activities			
Purchase of tangible fixed assets	(33,509)		(32,746)
Purchase of subsidiary undertakings (net of cash and cash equivalents acquired) (note 12)	(7,221)		(564)
Additional investment in associated undertaking	(850)		-
Decrease (increase) in loans to associated undertakings	576		(1,050)
Sale of fixed assets	1,293		1,410
Investment grants	644		-
Net cash outflow from investing activities		(39,067)	(32,950)
Net cash inflow before financing		4,287	1,332
Financing (note 24)			
Issue of Ordinary share capital	75,167		1,737
Net decrease in loans	(20,830)		(7,645)
Capital element of finance lease rental payments	(733)		(593)
Net cash inflow (outflow) from financing		53,604	(6,501)
Increase (decrease) in cash and cash equivalents (note 23)		57,891	(5,169)

Notes on pages 26 to 44 form part of these accounts.

Accounting Policies

1. Basis of accounts The accounts are prepared under the historical cost convention modified to include the revaluation of certain fixed assets and have been prepared in accordance with applicable accounting standards, including FRS 3.

2. Basis of consolidation The consolidated accounts include the accounts of the Company and its subsidiary undertakings and the Group's share of the results and post - acquisition reserves of associated undertakings. The results of the associated undertakings, adjusted as appropriate to accord with Group accounting policies, are included on the basis of audited accounts for a period ending not more than six months before 31 December. The net assets of subsidiary undertakings acquired during the year are incorporated at their fair value at the date of acquisition. Investments in associated undertakings acquired during the year are incorporated at the Group's share of fair value of underlying net assets at the date of acquisition. Any goodwill arising on acquisition is dealt with through distributable reserves, subject to merger relief available under the Companies Act 1985.

The results of subsidiary and associated undertakings acquired or disposed of in the year are included in the consolidated profit and loss account from the date of acquisition or up to the date of disposal. As permitted by Section 230 of the Companies Act 1985 the Company has not presented a separate profit and loss account.

3. Foreign currency transactions during the year are translated into sterling at the appropriate forward contract or rate of exchange at the date of transaction. Accounts of overseas subsidiary and associated undertakings in foreign currencies are translated into sterling using the year end exchange rates. Exchange differences arising from the translation of the opening balance sheets of subsidiary and associated undertakings are dealt with through reserves. Other gains and losses are included in the profit and loss account.

4. Stocks are valued at the lower of first - in, first - out cost and net realisable value; cost includes appropriate production overhead expenses.

5. Turnover represents the net amounts invoiced to external customers but excludes value added and sales taxes and any part of the sales of associated undertakings.

6. Leases Assets held under finance leases are capitalised as tangible fixed assets at fair value and the corresponding rentals liability is shown net of interest under finance leases within creditors. The capitalised values are written off over the shorter of the period of the lease and the useful life of the asset concerned and finance charges are written off over the period of the lease. Rental costs under operating leases are charged to the profit and loss account over the period of the lease.

7. Depreciation of tangible fixed assets is provided at rates estimated to write off the cost or valuation of assets over their useful lives, the principal rates of annual straight line depreciation being:

    a) Freehold buildings 2.5%. Freehold land is not depreciated.
    b) Leasehold land and buildings 2.5% or over the period of the lease if less than forty years.
    c) Plant between 10% and 33.33%.
    d) Vehicles between 16% and 25%.

8. Grants on assets are credited to the profit and loss account over the lives of the relevant assets. Other grants are credited to revenue in the year in which the expenditure to which they relate is charged.

9. Research and development, patents and trade marks expenditure is charged against profit of the year in which it is incurred.

10. Pension costs recorded in the year represent contributions payable under money purchase schemes and, in the case of final salary related schemes, the estimated regular cost of the benefits accruing during the year, adjusted to spread any variations from regular cost over the expected remaining working lives of employees, on a straight line basis. Differences between pension costs and contributions paid are recorded as assets or liabilities in the balance sheet.

11. Deferred taxation is provided using the liability method in respect of timing differences except where the liability is not expected to arise in the forseeable future. Advance corporation tax which is available to reduce the corporation tax payable on future profits is carried forward where recovery is reasonably assured and, to the extent appropriate, is deducted from the provision for deferred taxation.

Notes to the Accounts

£000

1 Segmental analysis	Turnover		Operating profit		Net assets	
Class of business	**1992**	1991	**1992**	1991	**1992**	1991
Cellular polymers	**518,175**	436,728	**32,141**	33,092	**132,001**	105,857
Industrial polymers	**162,769**	155,221	**7,620**	8,472	**38,218**	39,666
Fibres and fabrics	**104,545**	98,786	**6,374**	8,197	**28,700**	25,013
Corporate and other	**3,039**	3,541	**2,556**	3,577	**19,552**	19,019
	788,528	694,276	**48,691**	53,338	**218,471**	189,555
Geographical origin						
United Kingdom	**253,941**	242,896	**14,727**	15,921	**69,799**	66,471
Continental Europe	**499,427**	432,435	**33,340**	35,742	**138,400**	116,393
International	**35,160**	18,945	**624**	1,675	**10,272**	6,691
	788,528	694,276	**48,691**	53,338	**218,471**	189,555

Geographical destination		
United Kingdom	**230,358**	220,936
Benelux	**80,734**	63,698
France	**113,381**	97,446
Germany	**217,023**	194,224
Spain	**44,802**	44,319
Other	**48,553**	39,406
Continental Europe	**504,493**	439,093
International	**53,677**	34,247
	788,528	694,276

The share of profits of associated undertakings have been excluded from the segmental analysis and prior year figures have been adjusted accordingly.

Net assets comprise shareholders' funds, excluding investments, cash, borrowings and minority interests.

2   Operating profit
is stated after charging (crediting):

Depreciation	**25,001**	21,922
Hire and leasing of plant and vehicles	**3,043**	2,316
Auditors' remuneration	**769**	722
Research and development	**815**	710
Government grants	**(610)**	(248)

The Group auditors also received £28,000 in respect of non-audit services.

	£000	
3 Share of associated undertakings	**1992**	1991
Share of turnover	**83,645**	75,890
Share of profits less losses	**5,623**	1,624
Taxation (note 5)	**(1,525)**	(1,358)
	4,098	266
Less receivable as dividends	**(1,652)**	(1,643)
Retained by associated undertakings	**2,446**	(1,377)
4 Interest receivable (payable)		
Bank overdrafts, acceptance credits and bank loans	**(5,718)**	(9,311)
Finance leases	**(250)**	(231)
Loans not fully repayable within five years	**(878)**	(776)
Loan notes	**(254)**	(419)
	(7,100)	(10,737)
Less interest receivable	**7,942**	6,131
	842	(4,606)
5 Tax on profit on ordinary activities		
UK Corporation tax at 33% (33.25%)	**6,861**	3,553
Overseas tax	**13,528**	14,077
Associated undertakings (note 3)	**1,525**	1,358
Deferred taxation (note 18)	**(698)**	1,334
	21,216	20,322
6 Dividends		
Ordinary shares:		
Interim paid at 3.5p (3.34p, adjusted) per share	**7,483**	6,099
Final proposed at 3.65p (3.50p, adjusted) per share	**7,811**	6,375
4.2% Cumulative Preference shares	**2**	2
	15,296	12,476

7 Earnings per Ordinary share

The calculation of net earnings per 25p Ordinary share is based on earnings (after minority interests and Preference dividend) of £33,543,000 (£29,700,000) and on 206,376,573 (181,719,735 adjusted for the 1992 Rights Issue) shares, being the weighted average of Ordinary shares in issue during the year.

8 Employment costs

	1992	1991
Employees and directors:		
Wages and salaries	**161,623**	133,470
Social security costs	**27,544**	22,811
Other pension costs	**5,005**	4,950
	194,172	161,231

Average numbers employed:	1992	1991
UK	**4,005**	4,030
Continental Europe	**5,065**	4,896
International	**834**	732
Company and subsidiary undertakings	**9,904**	9,658
Associated undertakings	**2,842**	2,874
	12,746	12,532

9 Directors' emoluments

	1992	1991
Directors' emoluments including pension contributions:		
as directors	**54**	41
as executives:		
Salary and benefits	**893**	860
Performance related payments	**249**	291
Pension contributions	**356**	224
Pensions to former directors or their dependants	**18**	18
	1,570	1,434

£000

9 Directors' emoluments (continued)   **1992**   1991

Directors' emoluments, excluding pension contributions, include:
Chairman (and highest paid director) (including £Nil performance related)   **207**   268
Highest paid director (including £78,750 performance related)   **257**

The directors received emoluments, excluding pension contributions, in the following ranges:

			1992	1991
£15,001	-	£20,000	**2**	1
£25,001	-	£30,000	-	1
£35,001	-	£40,000	-	1
£140,001	-	£145,000	1	-
£155,001	-	£160,000	1	-
£160,001	-	£165,000	1	-
£190,001	-	£195,000	-	1
£195,001	-	£200,000	-	1
£205,001	-	£210,000	1	1
£230,001	-	£235,000	1	-
£240,001	-	£245,000	-	1
£255,001	-	£260,000	1	-
£265,001	-	£270,000	-	1

Executive directors' remuneration consists of a basic salary, reviewed annually by the Remuneration Committee, and a performance related bonus of a percentage of profits before taxation based on achievement of corporate performance targets set annually by the Remuneration Committee.

The above emolument figures do not include any amount for the value of share options granted to, or exercised by, directors, details of which are given below.

Directors' share options outstanding

Executive scheme	Adjusted price p	R. McGee	R.H. Sellers	F.J. Eaton	K.R. Bhatt	D.R. Hine	Total
Granted - 1984	34.598	-	72,417	71,684	-	143,071	287,172
Granted - 1987	122.664	-	-	-	31,794	-	31,794
Granted - 1988	137.902	-	-	-	31,036	-	31,036
Granted - 1990	179.143	-	31,036	-	-	-	31,036
Granted - 1992	237.000	-	-	-	25,000	-	25,000
Exercised in year		-	-	-	-	(143,071)	(143,071)
		-	103,453	71,684	87,830	-	262,967
Savings Related schemes							
Granted - 1987	117.758	3,140	940	1,570	-	-	5,650
Granted - 1988	122.372	-	940	2,352	1,469	-	4,761
Granted - 1989	149.630	-	673	-	1,202	-	1,875
Granted - 1990	126.045	2,855	2,855	3,426	2,855	8,568	20,559
Granted - 1991	180.174	2,080	2,288	1,039	2,080	-	7,487
Granted - 1992	229.600	4,899	3,266	3,266	3,266	-	13,880
Exercised in year		(3,140)	(940)	(1,570)	-	-	(5,650)
		9,834	10,022	9,266	10,872	8,568	48,562
Total at 31 December 1992		9,834	113,475	80,950	98,702	8,568	311,529

10 Pension arrangements

Vita companies continue to provide pension benefits for many employees by contributing to a variety of pension arrangements in addition to those provided by the State. In compliance with the Statement of Standard Accounting Practice No.24 (SSAP 24) 'Accounting for Pension Costs', the cost of these additional benefits is charged to the profit and loss account in the year in which they are incurred. Any difference between this charge and the actual contributions payable to external funds is shown on the balance sheet as an asset or liability.

Within the UK, the majority of employees are eligible to join one of the three schemes administered by British Vita Pensions Trust Limited which provide final salary related benefits from separately invested assets. The schemes are funded in accordance with the recommendations of the consultant actuaries, William M Mercer Limited. The members of the schemes are contracted-in to the State Earnings Related Pension Scheme but members have the option of contracting-out via a Rebate Only Personal Pension Scheme. All members receive an annual benefits statement, together with a copy of the Annual Report to members on the status of the appropriate scheme.

An actuarial valuation is undertaken every two years and the last valuation was performed at 31 March 1992 using the projected unit method to be consistent with the method used for the SSAP 24 valuation. The major assumptions were dividend growth of 4.5%, an interest rate of 9% and average remuneration increases of 7% per annum. The schemes were funded to a level between 100% and 129% of the accrued liabilities at the date of the valuation, after allowing for anticipated increases in remuneration levels. Schemes operated by British Vita Pensions Trust Limited held investments with a market value of £67,892,308 at 31 March 1992, including 2,710,692 Ordinary shares of British Vita PLC which then represented approximately 10% of two of the schemes' assets. The number of British Vita shares has subsequently been reduced to the current number of 1,960,692 as part of the transition arrangements to comply with new self-investment regulations. The main Vita schemes provide between 3% and 5% guaranteed indexation of current pensions, indexation in line with retail price index to a maximum of 5% of deferred pensions and apply equalised provisions for men and women. Separate, smaller final salary related schemes are also operated for certain other UK subsidiary companies. Recent actuarial valuations, completed with broadly similar assumptions but by consultant actuaries other than William M Mercer Limited, confirmed that these schemes were funded to a level exceeding 100% of the liabilities at the date of the valuation, after allowing for anticipated increases in remuneration levels and the benefit enhancement costs of completing their integration with the main Vita schemes.

Money-purchase schemes are operated in France, Holland, Belgium and Australia and employer contributions to these schemes are charged to the profit and loss account in the year in which they are payable.

A number of unfunded schemes are operated in Germany providing fixed amounts or final salary related benefits, for which reserves are created in accordance with the recommendations of the consultant actuary, International Pension Consultants GmbH. Actuarial valuations are undertaken every two years on the 'projected unit' method based on the major assumptions of a 7.5% per annum interest rate, remuneration increases of 4.5% per annum and increases to pensions in payment of 3.0% per annum. The last valuation, undertaken as of 31 December 1992, disclosed a deficit for which full provision has already been made.

Calculations have been performed for all final salary related schemes to comply with SSAP24 using the 'projected unit' method with similar assumptions to the main biennial valuations. It is the objective to fund pension arrangements by a substantially level contribution rate. The total pension charge for the year was £5,005,000 (£4,950,000) after deducting £431,000 (£857,000) in respect of the amortisation of surpluses arising in the UK over the average remaining service lives of employees in the various schemes.

£000

11 Tangible fixed assets		Group		Company
	Land & buildings	Plant & vehicles	Total	Plant & vehicles
Cost or valuation				
Balance 31 December 1991	104,459	222,186	326,645	332
Exchange rate adjustments	10,514	18,661	29,175	-
Additions	5,523	27,262	32,785	57
New subsidiary undertakings	2,402	5,912	8,314	-
Disposals	(405)	(7,077)	(7,482)	(78)
Revaluation	(6,889)	-	(6,889)	-
Balance 31 December 1992*	115,604	266,944	382,548	311
Accumulated depreciation				
Balance 31 December 1991	8,765	133,603	142,368	250
Exchange rate adjustments	957	11,849	12,806	-
New subsidiary undertakings	192	2,829	3,021	-
Disposals	(60)	(6,112)	(6,172)	(78)
Charge for year	2,644	22,357	25,001	43
Revaluation	(12,498)	-	(12,498)	-
Balance 31 December 1992	-	164,526	164,526	215
Net book value				
31 December 1992	115,604	102,418	218,022	96
31 December 1991	95,694	88,583	184,277	82
***Cost and valuation analysis:**				
Valuation 1992	115,604	-	115,604	-
Cost	-	266,944	266,944	311
	115,604	266,944	382,548	311

Land and buildings comprise:	
Freehold	110,030
Long leasehold buildings	2,373
Buildings subject to finance leases	3,201
	115,604

Valuation 1992

The freehold land and buildings and long leasehold properties of the Group were independently revalued as at the year end on an existing use basis by Dunlop Heywood & Co. Limited, Consultant Surveyors, with International subsidiaries being done in conjunction with local valuers. The valuation showed a surplus of £5,231,000 over the related net book values and this surplus has been credited to reserves. If land and buildings had not been revalued they would have been included at cost of £106,674,000 (£90,192,000) less accumulated depreciation of £24,034,000 (£21,040,000). Land at a valuation of £21,569,000 is not depreciated.

£000

12 Investments

	Group			Company		
	Associated undertakings Listed	Unlisted	Total	Subsidiary undertakings	Associated undertakings	Total
Shares at cost less amounts written off						
Balance 31 December 1991	9,388	904	10,292	68,171	375	68,546
Exchange rate and other adjustments	1,616	11	1,627	-	-	-
Additions	850	-	850	3,871	-	3,871
Reclassification to subsidiary undertaking	-	(154)	(154)	-	-	-
Balance 31 December 1992	11,854	761	12,615	72,042	375	72,417
Share of post acquisition reserves						
Balance 31 December 1991	(2,569)	8,001	5,432	-	-	-
Exchange rate adjustments	(844)	626	(218)	-	-	-
Reclassification to subsidiary undertaking	-	(748)	(748)	-	-	-
Share of retained profits	989	1,457	2,446	-	-	-
Balance 31 December 1992	(2,424)	9,336	6,912	-	-	-
Loans						
Balance 31 December 1991	-	1,150	1,150	17,335	1,150	18,485
Exchange rate adjustments	-	-	-	1,816	-	1,816
Advances	-	574	574	5,798	574	6,372
Repayments	-	(1,150)	(1,150)	(6,214)	(1,150)	(7,364)
Balance 31 December 1992	-	574	574	18,735	574	19,309
Net book value						
31 December 1992	9,430	10,671	20,101	90,777	949	91,726
31 December 1991	6,819	10,055	16,874	85,506	1,525	87,031
The market value of shares listed overseas and directors' valuation of unlisted shares in associated undertakings is:						
31 December 1992	18,418	21,000	39,418	-	14,000	14,000
31 December 1991	5,837	19,400	25,237	-	11,500	11,500

The directors' valuation of the investment in Spartech Corporation is based on the market value of the existing Common Stock holding and assumed conversion of the Convertible Preferred Stock holding.

Notes to the Accounts (continued)

£000

12 Investments (continued)

Details of acquisitions during the year are as follows:

Subsidiary undertakings

	1992	1991
Book values at acquisition:		
Tangible fixed assets and investments	5,293	8,841
Current assets:		
Stocks	2,022	1,717
Debtors	3,122	2,070
Cash at bank and in hand	728	296
Creditors due within one year:		
Bank loans and overdrafts	(1,730)	(93)
Other loans	(158)	(8,681)
Trade creditors	(2,366)	(1,783)
Other creditors and accruals	(2,094)	(447)
Creditors due after more than one year	(203)	(250)
Provisions for liabilities and charges	(282)	-
Minority interest acquired	(883)	-
Net assets acquired	3,449	1,670
Revaluations of tangible fixed assets	-	(1,000)
Fair value to the Group	3,449	670
Consideration paid:		
Cash	7,592	782
Reclassification of associated undertaking	902	-
Total	8,494	782
Goodwill paid	5,045	112

The subsidiary undertakings acquired during the year utilised £290,000 of (contributed £5,013,000 to) the Group's net operating cash flows, paid £195,000 (£360,000) in respect of net returns on investments and servicing of finance, paid £177,000 (£133,000) in respect of taxation and utilised £1,476,000 (£325,000) for investing activities

Analysis of the net outflow of cash and cash equivalents in respect of the purchase of subsidiary undertakings:

Cash consideration	7,592	782
Cash at bank and in hand acquired	(728)	(296)
Bank overdrafts of acquired subsidiary undertakings	357	78
Net outflow of cash and cash equivalents in respect of the purchase of subsidiary undertakings.	7,221	564

£000

13 Stocks	Group		Company	
	1992	1991	**1992**	1991
Raw materials and consumable stores	**38,102**	34,505	-	-
Work in progress and finished goods	**29,576**	24,986	-	-
	67,678	59,491	-	-

14 Debtors

Amounts falling due within one year

	Group		Company	
Trade debtors	**126,128**	114,522	-	-
Amounts owed by subsidiary undertakings	-	-	**19,380**	8,292
Amounts owed by associated undertakings	**2,255**	2,638	**655**	487
Other debtors	**5,685**	3,988	-	-
Prepayments and accrued income	**6,606**	5,616	**522**	147
Advance corporation tax	-	-	**1,563**	1,133
	140,674	126,764	**22,120**	10,059

Amounts falling due after more than one year

	Group		Company	
Other debtors	**592**	491	-	-
Advance corporation tax	-	-	**2,012**	2,125
	592	491	**2,012**	2,125

15 Creditors amounts falling due within one year:
Borrowings

	Group		Company	
Current portion of secured loans	**2,283**	3,077	-	-
Current portion of unsecured loans	**695**	7,770	-	-
Loans falling due within one year (note 17)	**2,978**	10,847	-	-
Bank overdrafts - unsecured	**23,150**	27,003	-	-
Bank overdrafts - secured	**142**	3,977	-	-
Loan notes - unsecured	**2,291**	3,454	**2,291**	3,454
Other loans - unsecured	**12**	6,278	-	-
Finance leases	**382**	574	-	-
	28,955	52,133	**2,291**	3,454

Others

	Group		Company	
Trade creditors	**101,863**	90,073	-	-
Bills payable	**7,564**	8,670	-	-
Amounts owed to subsidiary undertakings	-	-	**223**	-
Amounts owed to associated undertakings	**64**	168	-	-
Corporation tax	**23,470**	17,411	**4,381**	2,299
Other taxes and social security costs	**10,646**	10,408	**67**	15
Other creditors	**11,298**	10,661	**106**	513
Accruals and deferred income	**18,367**	15,314	**511**	438
Proposed dividend	**7,811**	6,375	**7,811**	6,375
	181,083	159,080	**13,099**	9,640

£000

16 Creditors amounts falling due after more than one year:	Group		Company	
	1992	1991	1992	1991
Borrowings				
Loans (note 17)	27,702	26,142	8,088	10,984
Finance leases	1,589	1,653	-	-
	29,291	27,795	8,088	10,984
Others				
Amounts owed to subsidiary undertakings	-	-	2,530	2,528
Corporation tax	-	106	-	-
Deferred income - government grants	1,107	855	-	-
Other creditors	1,130	1,178	18	18
	2,237	2,139	2,548	2,546
Finance lease obligations payable comprise:				
between one and two years	232	292	-	-
between two and five years	496	531	-	-
beyond five years	861	830	-	-
	1,589	1,653	-	-

17 Loans

Long term (not wholly repayable within five years)

Overseas:				
BFr bank loans 1993 - 1998	40	40	-	-
Dfl bank loans 1993 - 2012	2,120	-	-	-
Dm bank loans 1993 - 2001	2,550	1,682	-	-
FFr bank loans 1993 - 1998	175	357	-	-
Pts other loans 1993 - 2003	3,777	3,692	-	-

Medium term (repayable within five years)

UK:				
Bank loans 1993 - 1997	-	4,035	-	4,000
BFr bank loans 1993 - 1997	966	831	-	-
Dm bank loans 1993 - 1997	4,322	3,736	4,322	3,736
FFr bank loans 1993 - 1995	3,766	3,417	3,766	3,248

Overseas:				
A$ bank loan 1993 - 1994	68	96	-	-
BFr bank loans 1993 - 1997	30	130	-	-
Dm bank loans 1993 - 1997	2,182	8,152	-	-
Dfl bank loans 1993 - 1997	310	28	-	-
FFr bank loans 1993 - 1997	433	185	-	-
Pts other loans 1993 - 1997	9,941	10,608	-	-
	30,680	36,989	8,088	10,984

£000

17 Loans (continued)

	Group		Company	
	1992	1991	1992	1991
The loans are repayable as follows:				
between one and two years	4,592	4,579	-	-
between two and five years	18,672	18,361	8,088	10,984
beyond five years	4,438	3,202	-	-
Amounts falling due after more than one year (note 16)	27,702	26,142	8,088	10,984
Amounts falling due within one year (note 15)	2,978	10,847	-	-
	30,680	36,989	8,088	10,984

Interest charges on the Pts other loans are at fixed rates of interest not exceeding 10% and on the bank loans are linked to inter-bank rates relative to the currency borrowed, except for £229,000 of the Dm bank loans at fixed rates averaging 7.65%. All overseas loans are secured by fixed charges except for £920,000 of the Dm loans, £310,000 of the Dfl loans, £301,000 of the FFr loans and £3,487,000 of the Pts loans. The UK bank loans are unsecured.

18 Provisions for liabilities and charges

Group	Deferred taxation	Pensions	Other	Total
Balance 31 December 1991	5,658	11,395	1,836	18,889
Exchange rate adjustments	703	1,813	99	2,615
New subsidiaries	243	39	-	282
Charge (utilised) during the year	(698)	(1,380)	1,698	(380)
Advance corporation tax	777	-	-	777
Balance 31 December 1992	6,683	11,867	3,633	22,183

Company				
Balance 31 December 1991	82	250	-	332
Utilised during the year	-	(150)	-	(150)
Balance 31 December 1992	82	100	-	182

'Other' relates to rationalisation and redundancy provisions.

	Group		Company	
Provision for deferred taxation	1992	1991	1992	1991
Accelerated capital allowances	9,287	9,039	341	341
Advance corporation tax recoverable	(2,604)	(3,381)	(259)	(259)
	6,683	5,658	82	82

Notes to the Accounts (continued)

£000

18 Provisions for liabilities and charges (continued)	**Group**		**Company**	
	1992	1991	**1992**	1991
Full potential liability for deferred taxation				
Accelerated capital allowances	**11,602**	11,006	**341**	341
Advance corporation tax recoverable	**(2,604)**	(3,381)	**(259)**	(259)
	8,998	7,625	**82**	82

No capital gains tax provision has been made in respect of the revaluation surplus on properties which are held for long term use.

19 Called up share capital

	Authorised		Allotted, called up and fully paid	
4.2% Cumulative Preference shares of £1 each (60,000 authorised, 57,450 allotted)	**60**	60	**57**	57
Ordinary shares of 25p each (300,000,000 authorised, 213,926,954 allotted)	**75,000**	60,000	**53,482**	44,270
	75,060	60,060	**53,539**	44,327

On 4 March 1992, the Company announced a fully underwritten 1 for 5 Rights Issue resulting in the issue of 35,416,471 new Ordinary shares of 25p nominal value, at a price of 212p each, to provide financing for future acquisitions and investments.

During the year, 1,353,649 Ordinary shares were allotted and issued, fully paid, in accordance with the rules of the share option schemes and 80,609 Ordinary shares were allotted and issued, fully paid, to subscribers to the Vita PEPs.

Employee share options

Employee participation in the Company continues to be successfully encouraged by means of share option schemes. At 31 December 1992, the British Vita Savings Related Share Option Schemes had 3,901 options outstanding over 5,220,421 shares at prices between 122.37p and 229.6p, including 1,201 options outstanding over 1,445,280 shares granted in May 1992 at 229.6p. Options under this scheme are exercisable on the fifth anniversary of the grant and, to December 1992, options had been exercised over 2,218,520 shares.

The Vita International Savings Related Share Option Scheme was introduced during 1990 and at 31 December 1992 there were 243 options outstanding over 435,854 shares at prices of between 139.19p and 229.6p, including 129 options over 200,773 shares granted in May 1992 at 229.6p.

The 1984 British Vita Executive and International Share Option Schemes had 349 options outstanding at 31 December 1992 over 3,989,653 shares at prices between 34.6p and 237p, including 95 options over 520,500 shares granted in April 1992 at 237p and 20 options over 106,300 shares issued in October 1992 at 220p per share. Options under these schemes are exercisable between the third and tenth anniversary of the grant and, by December 1992, options had been exercised over 4,438,867 shares.

At 31 December 1992, a further 5,089,381 shares were available for future grants of options under the current schemes.

20 Reserves

Group	Share premium	Revaluation reserve	Other reserves	Profit and loss
Balance 31 December 1991	15,273	11,912	3,034	97,723
Exchange rate adjustments	-	355	(56)	15,405
Premium on issues of shares	65,955	-	-	-
Goodwill on acquisitions	-	-	-	(5,045)
Realised revaluation gains	-	(81)	-	81
Property revaluation surplus	-	5,231	-	-
Retained profit for the financial year	-	-	-	18,249
Other movements	-	-	668	(668)
Balance 31 December 1992	81,228	17,417	3,646	125,745
Including reserves of associated undertakings				
1992	-	10	1,016	5,886
1991	-	18	684	4,730

Company

	Share premium	Revaluation reserve	Other reserves	Profit and loss
Balance 31 December 1991	15,273	-	9,440	14,210
Premium on issues of shares	65,955	-	-	-
Retained profit for the financial year	-	-	-	3,213
Balance 31 December 1992	81,228	-	9,440	17,423

The cumulative amount of goodwill resulting from acquisitions in the current and earlier financial years which has been written off was £24,772,000 (£19,727,000).

Of the total reserves shown in the Balance Sheets, the profit and loss account reserves are regarded as distributable.

21 Capital and leasing commitments

Commitments for capital expenditure at 31 December 1992 not provided for in the accounts amounted to £3,148,000 (£4,846,581) for the Group and £ Nil (£Nil) for the Company. In addition capital expenditure authorised by the directors but not contracted amounted to £5,271,000 (£264,000) for the Group and £Nil (£Nil) for the Company.

The Group has annual commitments in respect of operating leases expiring:

	Land and building	Plant and vehicles
Within one year	134	921
Between one and five years	728	4,015
Beyond five years	834	188
	1,696	5,124

During the year the Group entered into finance lease arrangements in respect of assets with a total capital value at the inception of the leases of £138,000 (£626,000).

£000

22 Reconciliation of operating profit to net cash inflow from operating activities	1992	1991
Operating profit	48,691	53,338
Depreciation charges	25,001	21,922
Loss (profit) on sale of tangible fixed assets	17	(372)
Government grants	(610)	(248)
Increase (decrease) in provisions	318	(288)
(Increase) decrease in stocks	(210)	2,369
Increase in debtors	(1,088)	(1,741)
Decrease in creditors	(968)	(5,523)
Net cash inflow from operating activities	71,151	69,457

23 Analysis of changes in cash and cash equivalents during the year

		1992	1991
Balance 31 December 1991		14,788	19,816
Net cash inflow (outflow) before adjustments for the effect of foreign exchange rate changes		57,891	(5,169)
Effect of foreign exchange rate changes		5,277	141
Movement in cash and cash equivalents (see below)		63,168	(5,028)
Balance 31 December 1992		77,956	14,788

	Movement in year		
Cash at bank and short term investments	55,480	101,248	45,768
Bank overdrafts	7,688	(23,292)	(30,980)
	63,168	77,956	14,788

£000

24 Analysis of changes in financing during the year	1992		1991	
	Share capital (inc premium)	Loans and finance lease obligations	Share capital (inc premium)	Loans and finance lease obligations
Balance 31 December 1991	59,600	48,948	57,863	46,825
Effect of foreign exchange rate changes	-	5,900		789
Cash flows from financing	75,167	(21,563)	1,737	(8,238)
Loans and finance lease obligations of subsidiary undertakings acquired during year	-	1,531	-	8,946
Inception of finance lease contracts	-	138	-	626
Balance 31 December 1992	134,767	34,954	59,600	48,948

25 Contingencies

The Company has guaranteed certain of the overdrafts and third party liabilities of certain subsidiary undertakings, amounting to £16,810,000 (£29,673,000).

In addition to pension liabilities referred to in note 10, there were contingent liabilities in respect of discounted bills of exchange totalling £3,432,000 (£2,909,000) for the Group.

An action is being pursued in the USA against the Company and certain directors in relation to, and involving, Spartech Corporation, which is being vigorously defended as the directors are advised and believe there to be no merit in the claim.

Principal Subsidiary and Associated Undertakings

Subsidiary undertakings	Country of incorporation and principal operation	Product or activities
United Kingdom		
Ball & Young Limited	England	Cellular polymer products
British Vita Investments Limited	England	Property management
Caligen Foam Limited	England	Cellular polymer products
Kay - Metzeler Limited	England	Cellular polymer products
Royalite Plastics Limited	Scotland	Polymeric products
The Rossendale Combining Company Limited	England	Specialised textiles
Vitacom Limited	England	Polymeric compounds
Vitafoam Limited	England	Cellular polymer products
Vitafibres Limited	England	Fibre processing
Vitamol Limited	England	Polymeric products
Vita Industrial Polymers Limited	England	Polymeric products
Vita Liquid Polymers Limited	England	Polymeric compounds
Vita International Limited	England	Parent company
Vita Services Limited	England	Administrative services
Vita - tex Limited	England	Specialised textiles
Continental Europe		
Caligen Europe BV	Netherlands	Cellular polymer products
Deutsche Vita Polymere GmbH	Germany	Parent company
Draka Interfoam BV	Netherlands	Cellular polymer products
ICOA SA	Spain	Cellular polymer products
ICOA France SA (66%)	France	Cellular polymer products
ICOA Levante SA	Spain	Cellular polymer products
Isofel SA (67.5%)	Spain	Cellular polymer products
Koepp AG (94.25%)	Germany	Cellular polymer products
Ledikanten-en Matrassen Fabriek Oost BV	Netherlands	Cellular polymer products
Libeltex AB	Sweden	Fibre processing
Libeltex GmbH	Germany	Fibre processing

Subsidiary undertakings	Country of incorporation and principal operation	Product or activities
Libeltex NV	Belgium	Fibre processing
Metzeler Laminados Iberia SA (93.92%)	Spain	Polymeric products
Metzeler Mousse SA	France	Cellular polymer products
Metzeler Plastics GmbH	Germany	Polymeric products
Metzeler Schaum GmbH	Germany	Cellular polymer products
Morard Europe SA	France	Cellular polymer products
Norma Boxmeer BV	Netherlands	Cellular polymer products
Poly-Kunststoffverarbeitung GmbH	Germany	Cellular polymer products
Radium Foam BV	Netherlands	Cellular polymer products
Radium Latex GmbH	Germany	Cellular polymer products
Roon SA	France	Polymeric products
Royalite Plastics SRL	Italy	Polymeric products
J. Schmidt Schaumstoffe GmbH	Germany	Cellular polymer products
Tramico SA	France	Cellular polymer products
Unifoam AG	Switzerland	Patent licensing
Veenendaal en Co BV	Netherlands	Cellular polymer products
Veenendaal Schaumstoffwerk GmbH	Germany	Cellular polymer products
Vitafoam Europe BV	Netherlands	Parent company
Vita Interfoam BV	Netherlands	Parent company
Vita Polymers Denmark A/S	Denmark	Polymeric products
Vita Polymers Europe BV	Netherlands	Parent company
Vita Polymeres France SA	France	Parent company
Vita Polymers Poland Sp.zo.o	Poland	Cellular polymer products

International

RLA Polymers Pty. Limited	Australia	Polymeric compounds
Vitafoam CA (Private) Limited	Zimbabwe	Cellular polymer products
Vitafoam Incorporated	USA	Cellular polymer products

| Associated undertakings | Country of incorporation and principal operation | Equity | | |
		Total 000's	Company interest %	Results up to
United Kingdom				
BTR - Vitaline Limited	England	£350	50	31 Dec
Emotex Trading Company Limited	England	£1	50	31 Dec
Vita - Achter Limited	England	£400	50	31 Dec
Continental Europe				
Vita Cortex Holdings Limited	Ireland	IR£529	50	31 Dec
International				
Spartech Corporation	USA	US$2,945	24	31 Oct
Taki - Vita SAE	Egypt	E£8,000	40	31 Dec
Vita Inoac Limited	Japan	Y63,000	20	30 Jun
Vitafoam Nigeria PLC	Nigeria	N18,200	20	30 Sep
Vitafoam Products Canada Limited	Canada	C$20	50	30 Sep

Notes:

1. Unless otherwise indicated 100% of issued share capital is owned by British Vita PLC. Interests in the Continental European and International subsidiary undertakings are held through subsidiary undertakings of British Vita PLC, the ultimate Parent Company.

2. Interests in BTR - Vitaline Limited, Emotex Trading Company Limited and Vita - Achter Limited are held directly by British Vita PLC. All other associated undertakings are held through subsidiary undertakings of British Vita PLC.

3. The principal activity of the associated undertakings is the manufacture and processing of polymers.

4. Vita International Limited also holds 100% of the 373,500 Series L Cumulative 6% Convertible Preferred Stock of Spartech Corporation and, indirectly, 50% of the IR£10,572 preference shares of Vita Cortex Holdings Limited.

5. Vitafoam Nigeria PLC and Spartech Corporation are listed, respectively, on the Nigerian and American Stock Exchanges.

6. The accounts of all subsidiary undertakings, except the ICOA SA, ICOA Levante SA, Ledikanten-en Matrassen Fabriek Oost BV, Norma Boxmeer BV, Roon SA and Vitafoam CA (Private) Limited, are audited by Arthur Andersen. The accounts of all associated undertakings, except Spartech Corporation, are audited by firms other than Arthur Andersen.

Directors' Responsibility Statement

The directors acknowledge that it is their responsibility to:

i) prepare, for the Company and the Group, a profit and loss account which gives a true and fair view of the profit and loss for the year ended 31 December 1992, and

ii) prepare, for the Company and the Group, a balance sheet which gives a true and fair view of the state of affairs as at 31 December 1992, and

iii) prepare such accounts in accordance with appropriate accounting policies and standards, consistently applied and supported by reasonable and prudent judgements or estimates, and

iv) maintain adequate accounting records, an effective system of internal controls and internal audit to assist in the prevention and detection of fraud or other irregularities, and

v) safeguard the assets of the Group.

The directors believe that the Report and Accounts for 1992 has been prepared in line with the above responsibilities.

Auditors' Report

Auditors' report to the Members of British Vita PLC

We have audited the accounts on pages 22 to 44 in accordance with Auditing Standards.

In our opinion the accounts give a true and fair view of the state of affairs of the Company and the Group at 31 December 1992 and of the profit and cash flows of the Group and of the total recognised gains and losses of the Company and the Group for the year then ended and have been properly prepared in accordance with the Companies Act 1985.

Arthur Andersen

Arthur Andersen   9 March 1993
Chartered Accountants and Registered Auditor
Bank House, 9 Charlotte Street, Manchester M1 4EU.

Notice of Meeting

Notice is hereby given that the Twenty - seventh Annual General Meeting of British Vita PLC will be held at the British Vita Training and Development Centre, Green Street, Middleton, Manchester on Wednesday 14 April 1993 at 2.15pm for the following purposes:

Ordinary business

1. To receive and consider the accounts and the reports of the directors and auditors for the year ended 31 December 1992.

2. To confirm the dividends paid and to declare a final dividend on the Ordinary shares for the year ended 31 December 1992.

3. To re-appoint Mr L.D. Lawton as a director.

4. That in accordance with Section 293 (5) of the Companies Act 1985, Mr J.H. Ogden, despite having attained the age of 71, be re-appointed a director.

5. That in accordance with Section 293(5) of the Companies Act 1985, Mr F. A. Parker, despite having attained the age of 73, be re-appointed a director.

6. To re-appoint Arthur Andersen as auditors of the Company and to authorise the directors to fix their remuneration.

Special business

To consider and, if thought fit, pass the following resolution which will be proposed as a special resolution:

7. That the directors be and they are hereby empowered in accordance with Section 95 of the Companies Act 1985 ("the Act") to allot equity securities (within the meaning of Section 94(2) of the Act) pursuant to the general authority conferred upon them as if Section 89(1) of the Act did not apply to any such allotment so that:

    (i) reference to allotment in this resolution shall be construed in accordance with Section 94(3) of the Act; and

    (ii) the power conferred by this resolution shall enable the Company to make any offer or agreement before the expiry of the period stated in sub-paragraph (b) below which would or might require equity securities to be allotted after the expiry of such period and the directors may allot equity securities in pursuance of any such offer or agreement notwithstanding the expiry of the power conferred hereby;

PROVIDED, however, that the power conferred by this resolution shall:

(a) be limited:

    (i) to the allotment of equity securities which are offered to all the holders of issued Ordinary shares of

46

the Company (at a date selected by the directors) where the equity securities respectively attributable to the holders of all Ordinary shares are as nearly as practicable in proportion to the number of Ordinary shares held by them but subject to such exclusions and other arrangements as the directors may deem necessary or expedient in relation to fractional entitlements and any legal or practical difficulties under the laws of any overseas territory or the requirements of any regulatory body or stock exchange;

(ii) to the allotment (otherwise than pursuant to sub-paragraph (a) (i) above) of equity securities up to an aggregate nominal amount of £1,875,000; and

(b) expire on whichever is the earlier of 15 months from the passing of this resolution and the date of the Twenty-eighth Annual General Meeting of the Company except to the extent that the same is renewed or extended on or before that date.

By order of the Board
A.R. Teague
Secretary

Oldham Road, Middleton
Manchester, M24 2DB

18 March 1993

An Ordinary shareholder entitled to attend and vote is entitled to appoint one or more proxies (whether members or not) to attend and, on a poll, vote instead of himself. A form of proxy must reach the Company's Registrar, National Westminster Bank Plc, by 9.30am on Tuesday 13 April. A form of proxy is included for the use of Ordinary shareholders, completion of which does not prevent an Ordinary shareholder from personally attending the meeting.

Copies of the directors' contracts of service and the rules of the Company's share option schemes will be available for inspection at the Registered Office of the Company on any weekday (public holidays excepted) during normal business hours from the date of this Notice until the date of the meeting and, at the place of the meeting, for a period of fifteen minutes prior to and during the meeting.

Shareholder Information

Registered office

Oldham Road, Middleton,
Manchester M24 2DB
(Registered in England No. 871669)

Auditors

Arthur Andersen
Chartered Accountants,
9 Charlotte Street,
Manchester M1 4EU

Principal bankers

National Westminster Bank Plc
Lloyds Bank Plc
Deutsche Bank AG

Registrar and share transfer office

National Westminster Bank Plc
Registrar's Department,
Bristol BS99 7NH

Financial Calendar

Preliminary announcement of results for financial year	Early March
Report and Accounts circulated	Late March
Annual General Meeting	Mid April
Interim Report	Mid September
Dividend payments	
Interim	Mid November
Final	Mid May

Appendix D. 1993 Interim Report
of British Vita PLC

Chairman's Statement

Results

Performance in this first half has been dominated by the volume and margin pressures which we have felt across most of our operations reflecting particularly the continued recessionary conditions of European economies. Continental Europe has been especially affected with sales levels decreasing, in local currency terms, in comparison with the same period last year. The worsening conditions in Spain led us to divest our Icoa SA operations towards the end of the half-year, the associated losses and divestment cost totalling just over £6m being included in these results. Further rationalisation is being considered in certain other businesses in Germany and Spain.

Despite achieving consistently high levels of efficiency throughout our operations, in the current market conditions it is important to continue with the cost reduction programmes to which I referred earlier in the year. These are currently concentrated in Continental Europe where a reduction of 7% in numbers employed, excluding divestments and acquisitions, will have been achieved by the end of this year.

Although the long awaited recovery in the UK shows little effect to date, our UK companies have achieved a 25% improvement in export sales compared with the first half of last year and there have been commendable performances from our fibres and fabrics operations. The results of our North American companies are also showing an upward trend as the recovery in the economy there becomes more apparent.

Opportunities have been taken for further developments, especially through two acquisitions in France which have strengthened our involvement in engineering thermoplastics (J. Gaillon SA) and specialist rubber and cellular plastics conversion (Pullflex SA). These acquisitions, together with other smaller businesses acquired in the USA and the UK and our continued developments in Poland, involved investment totalling over £18m in the period.

The Balance Sheet remains strong with net cash at similar levels to the year-end after the benefit of reduced borrowings following the Spanish divestment but offset by costs of our acquisitions and capital expenditure programme.

Dividend

The Board has declared an interim dividend of 3.65p (3.5p) payable on 8 November 1993 to shareholders on the Register at the close of business on 8 October 1993.

Board

Mr Alan Jones was appointed as a non-executive director on 19 May 1993 and, after a suitable transition period, Mr James Ogden has today retired as a non-executive director after almost 26 years excellent service in that role and 39 years as a legal consultant to the company.

Future

Whilst constantly pursuing product and technical innovations, the emphasis in the short term remains focused on controlling costs especially in Germany, the area most affected by the depressed economic conditions in Europe. An immediate concern throughout all our cellular polymers operations is recovery of significant raw material cost increases which were imposed in the third quarter and which will be recovered only with difficulty later this year.

Nevertheless, with a strongly motivated team and an excellent asset base supported by continued good levels of investment for productivity and technological leadership, we are confident of maintaining our leading position in our chosen markets across the whole of Europe and obtaining further improvements in our International operations.

6 September 1993

R. McGee

Consolidated Profit and Loss Account
for the six months ended 30 June 1993

Year 1992	£000	First half 1993	1992
	Turnover (Note 3)		
684,360	**Continuing operations**	**381,557**	345,397
19,056	**Acquisitions**	**10,049**	9,072
703,416		**391,606**	354,469
33,805	**Discontinued operations**	**12,820**	18,483
737,221		**404,426**	372,952
	Operating profit (Note 3)		
48,771	**Continuing operations**	**19,194**	24,962
713	**Acquisitions**	**313**	424
49,484		**19,507**	25,386
(3,411)	**Discontinued operations**	**(2,052)**	(854)
46,073	**Operating profit**	**17,455**	24,532
5,380	**Share of profit of associated undertakings**	**2,449**	3,063
51,453		**19,904**	27,595
-	**Loss on disposal of discontinued operations**	**(3,545)**	
51,453	**Profit before interest**	**16,359**	27,595
867	**Net interest receivable (payable)**	**(99)**	(744)
52,320	**Profit on ordinary activities before taxation**	**16,260**	26,851
(19,860)	**Tax on profit on ordinary activities**	**(7,457)**	(10,874)
32,460	**Profit on ordinary activities after taxation**	**8,803**	15,977
(346)	**Minority interests**	**(285)**	(215)
32,114	**Profit for the period**	**8,518**	15,762
(15,296)	**Dividends**	**(7,858)**	(7,483)
16,818	**Retained profit**	**660**	8,279
15.6p	**Earnings per share**	**4.0p**	7.9p
7.15p	**Dividend per share**	**3.65p**	3.5p

Group Balance Sheet

(abridged) as at 30 June 1993

31 December 1992	£000	30 June 1993	1992
238,123	**Fixed assets**	**226,544**	206,490
	Current assets		
67,678	Stocks	**68,331**	63,924
141,266	Debtors	**148,052**	140,489
101,248	Cash at bank and short term investments	**88,199**	116,173
310,192		**304,582**	320,586
	Liabilities and provisions		
(58,246)	Borrowings	**(44,406)**	(76,070)
(183,320)	Others	**(189,060)**	(182,738)
(22,183)	Provisions for liabilities and charges	**(20,998)**	(18,586)
(263,749)		**(254,464)**	(277,394)
284,566		**276,662**	249,682
	Represented by:		
281,575	Capital and reserves	**273,888**	248,018
2,991	Minority interests	**2,774**	1,664
284,566		**276,662**	249,682
132p	Net assets per share	**128p**	116p
(15%)	Gearing (Net cash)	**(16%)**	(16%)

Notes

1. The company's accounting policy for translation of the results of the overseas subsidiary and associated undertakings has been changed from applying fixed exchange rates at period ends to average of the exchange rates during the period. The published figures for 1992 have been restated in accordance with this policy.

2. The figures for the six months ended 30 June 1993 and the comparatives for the six months ended 30 June 1992 are non-statutory accounts within the meaning of Section 240 of the Companies Act 1985 and are unaudited. The results for the financial year ended 31 December 1992 are an abridged version of the published accounts, subject to note 1, which have been reported on without qualification by the auditors and have been delivered to the Registrar of Companies.

3. Segmental analysis

£000	Turnover			Operating profit		
	First half		Year	First half		Year
	1993	1992	1992	1993	1992	1992
Class of business						
Cellular polymers	250,095	223,003	444,343	12,781	16,392	32,680
Industrial polymers	84,052	80,062	155,310	1,757	3,932	7,117
Fibres and fabrics	55,664	49,786	100,863	3,425	3,361	5,976
Corporate and other	1,795	1,618	2,900	1,544	1,701	3,711
	391,606	354,469	703,416	19,507	25,386	49,484
Discontinued	12,820	18,483	33,805	(2,052)	(854)	(3,411)
	404,426	372,952	737,221	17,455	24,532	46,073
Geographical origin						
United Kingdom	135,222	126,757	253,941	6,704	8,147	16,003
Continental Europe	237,026	212,707	418,491	12,376	16,922	32,870
International	19,358	15,005	30,984	427	317	611
	391,606	354,469	703,416	19,507	25,386	49,484
Discontinued	12,820	18,483	33,805	(2,052)	(854)	(3,411)
	404,426	372,952	737,221	17,455	24,532	46,073
Geographical destination						
United Kingdom	121,656	115,620	230,043			
Continental Europe	236,684	215,210	424,781			
International	33,266	23,639	48,592			
	391,606	354,469	703,416			
Discontinued	12,820	18,483	33,805			
	404,426	372,952	737,221			

Index

Visit Penguin on the Internet
and browse at your leisure

- ◆ preview sample extracts of our forthcoming books
- ◆ read about your favourite authors
- ◆ investigate over 10,000 titles
- ◆ enter one of our literary quizzes
- ◆ win some fantastic prizes in our competitions
- ◆ e-mail us with your comments and book reviews
- ◆ instantly order any Penguin book

and masses more!

'To be recommended without reservation ... a rich and rewarding on-line experience' – Internet Magazine

www.penguin.co.uk

READ MORE IN PENGUIN

In every corner of the world, on every subject under the sun, Penguin represents quality and variety – the very best in publishing today.

For complete information about books available from Penguin – including Puffins, Penguin Classics and Arkana – and how to order them, write to us at the appropriate address below. Please note that for copyright reasons the selection of books varies from country to country.

In the United Kingdom: Please write to *Dept. EP, Penguin Books Ltd, Bath Road, Harmondsworth, West Drayton, Middlesex UB7 ODA*

In the United States: Please write to *Consumer Sales, Penguin USA, P.O. Box 999, Dept. 17109, Bergenfield, New Jersey 07621-0120*. VISA and MasterCard holders call 1-800-253-6476 to order Penguin titles

In Canada: Please write to *Penguin Books Canada Ltd, 10 Alcorn Avenue, Suite 300, Toronto, Ontario M4V 3B2*

In Australia: Please write to *Penguin Books Australia Ltd, P.O. Box 257, Ringwood, Victoria 3134*

In New Zealand: Please write to *Penguin Books (NZ) Ltd, Private Bag 102902, North Shore Mail Centre, Auckland 10*

In India: Please write to *Penguin Books India Pvt Ltd, 706 Eros Apartments, 56 Nehru Place, New Delhi 110 019*

In the Netherlands: Please write to *Penguin Books Netherlands bv, Postbus 3507, NL-1001 AH Amsterdam*

In Germany: Please write to *Penguin Books Deutschland GmbH, Metzlerstrasse 26, 60594 Frankfurt am Main*

In Spain: Please write to *Penguin Books S. A., Bravo Murillo 19, 1° B, 28015 Madrid*

In Italy: Please write to *Penguin Italia s.r.l., Via Felice Casati 20, I–20124 Milano*

In France: Please write to *Penguin France S. A., 17 rue Lejeune, F–31000 Toulouse*

In Japan: Please write to *Penguin Books Japan, Ishikiribashi Building, 2–5–4, Suido, Bunkyo-ku, Tokyo 112*

In South Africa: Please write to *Longman Penguin Southern Africa (Pty) Ltd, Private Bag X08, Bertsham 2013*

READ MORE IN PENGUIN

BUSINESS

READ MORE IN PENGUIN

BUSINESS AND ECONOMICS

The Affluent Society   John Kenneth Galbraith

Classical economics was born in a harsh world of mass poverty, and it has
left us with a set of preoccupations hard to adapt to the realities of our own
richer age. Our unfamiliar problems need a new approach, and the
reception given to this famous book has shown the value of its fresh, lively
ideas.

Understanding the British Economy
Peter Donaldson and John Farquhar

A comprehensive and well-signposted tour of the British economy today;
a sound introduction to elements of economic theory; and a balanced
account of recent policies are provided by this bestselling text.

A Question of Economics   Peter Donaldson

Twenty key issues – the City, trade unions, 'free market forces' and many
others – are presented clearly and fully in this major book based on a
television series.

The Economics of the Common Market   Dennis Swann

From the CAP to the EMS, this is an internationally recognized book on
the Common Market – now substantially revised.

The Money Machine: How the City Works   Philip Coggan

How are the big deals made? Which are the institutions that really matter?
What causes the pound to rise or interest rates to fall? This book provides
clear and concise answers to these and many other money-related
questions.

Parkinson's Law   C. Northcote Parkinson

'Work expands so as to fill the time available for its completion': that law
underlies this 'extraordinarily funny and witty book' (Stephen Potter in the
Sunday Times) which also makes some painfully serious points about
those in business or the Civil Service.

READ MORE IN PENGUIN

BUSINESS AND ECONOMICS

From Boom to Bust David Smith

When Margaret Thatcher took office for the third time in 1987 her monetarist experiment had been replaced by more pragmatic policies, inflation and unemployment were both low, and there was even talk of an 'economic miracle'. By 1991 this short-lived boom was just a distant memory.

Atlas of Management Thinking Edward de Bono

This fascinating book provides a vital repertoire of non-verbal images that will help activate the right side of any manager's brain.

Almost Everyone's Guide to Economics
J. K. Galbraith and Nicole Salinger

This instructive and entertaining dialogue provides a step-by-step explanation of 'the state of economics in general and the reasons for its present failure in particular, in simple, accurate language that everyone could understand and that a perverse few might conceivably enjoy'.

The Economist Economics Rupert Pennant-Rea and Clive Crook

Based on a series of 'briefs' published in *The Economist* , this is a clear and accessible guide to the key issues of today's economics for the general reader.

The Rise and Fall of Monetarism David Smith

Now that even Conservatives have consigned monetarism to the scrap heap of history, David Smith draws out the unhappy lessons of a fundamentally flawed economic experiment, driven by a doctrine that for years had been regarded as outmoded and irrelevant.

Understanding Organizations Charles B. Handy

Of practical as well as theoretical interest, this book shows how general concepts can help solve specific organizational problems.

READ MORE IN PENGUIN

POLITICS AND SOCIAL SCIENCES

National Identity   Anthony D. Smith

In this stimulating new book, Anthony D. Smith asks why the first modern nation states developed in the West. He considers how ethnic origins, religion, language and shared symbols can provide a sense of nation and illuminates his argument with a wealth of detailed examples.

The Feminine Mystique   Betty Friedan

'A brilliantly researched, passionately argued book – a time-bomb flung into the Mom-and-Apple-Pie image ... Out of the debris of that shattered ideal, the Women's Liberation Movement was born' – Ann Leslie

Peacemaking Among Primates   Frans de Waal

'A vitally fresh analysis of the biology of aggression which deserves the serious attention of all those concerned with the nature of conflict, whether in humans or non-human animals ... De Waal delivers forcibly and clearly his interpretation of the significance of his findings ... Lucidly written' – The Times Higher Educational Supplement

Political Ideas   David Thomson (ed.)

From Machiavelli to Marx – a stimulating and informative introduction to the last 500 years of European political thinkers and political thought.

The Raw and the Cooked   Claude Lévi-Strauss

Deliberately, brilliantly and inimitably challenging, Lévi-Strauss's seminal work of structural anthropology cuts wide and deep into the mind of mankind, as he finds in the myths of the South American Indians a comprehensible psychological pattern.

The Social Construction of Reality
Peter Berger and Thomas Luckmann

The Social Construction of Reality is concerned with the sociology of 'everything that passes for knowledge in society', and particularly with that 'common-sense knowledge' that constitutes the reality of everyday life for the ordinary member of society.

READ MORE IN PENGUIN

POLITICS AND SOCIAL SCIENCES

Conservatism   Ted Honderich

'It offers a powerful critique of the major beliefs of modern conservatism, and shows how much a rigorous philosopher can contribute to understanding the fashionable but deeply ruinous absurdities of his times' – *New Statesman & Society*

Karl Marx: Selected Writings in Sociology and Social Philosophy   Bottomore and Rubel (eds.)

'It makes available, in coherent form and lucid English, some of Marx's most important ideas. As an introduction to Marx's thought, it has very few rivals indeed' – *British Journal of Sociology*

Post-War Britain   A Political History   Alan Sked and Chris Cook

Major political figures from Attlee to Thatcher, the aims and achievements of governments and the changing fortunes of Britain in the period since 1945 are thoroughly scrutinized in this stimulating history.

Inside the Third World   Paul Harrison

This comprehensive book brings home a wealth of facts and analysis on the often tragic realities of life for the poor people and communities of Asia, Africa and Latin America.

Medicine, Patients and the Law   Margaret Brazier

'An absorbing book which, in addition to being accessible to the general reader, should prove illuminating for practitioners – both medical and legal – and an ideal accompaniment to student courses on law and medicine' – *New Law Journal*

Bread and Circuses   Paul Veyne

'Warming oneself at the fire of M. Veyne's intelligence is such a joy that any irritation at one's prejudice and ignorance being revealed and exposed vanishes with his winning ways ... *Bread and Circuses* is M. Veyne's way of explaining the philosophy of the Roman Empire, which was the most successful form of government known to mankind' – *Literary Review*